EMBRACING ERRICKA

MY JOURNEY FROM FEAR TO FAITH

by Erricka Willard

Foreword by Amy Vossen Vukelic

Utilizing my conflicting truths and heartfelt inspirational reflections to heal and connect God's family

RPSS Publishing - Buffalo, New York

Copyright © 2024 by Erricka Willard

All rights reserved.

www.rpsspublishing.com

All rights reserved. No part of this publication may be reproduced or
distributed in any form or by any means, or stored in a database or retrieval
system, without the prior written permission of the publisher.

publisher@rockpapersafetyscissors.com
Embracing Erricka - My Journey from Fear to Faith
Paperback
ISBN:978-1-956688-37-5
Printed in the United States of America
First Edition

10 9 8 7 6 5 4 3 2 1

To my Heavenly Father,
to You be the glory.

Thank you for blessing me with the ability to write this book. Thank You for inspiring me to give love to thousands, maybe even millions, of people who are stuck in life, waking in a state of fear, unsure of what to do in their lives.

My wish is to transform millions of lives: moving people from fear to faith and understanding and bringing healing, embracing, and allowing the love of self first.

Contents

FOREWORD

When Erricka told me that she was spending so much time writing her book, I felt excited for her and those of us who would be blessed to read it.

I met Erricka in 2013 through our shared passion for Restorative Practices, whereby each person who chooses to "sit in a circle" gets the opportunity to share our truths, stories, and positions without interruption, judgment, or debate. I have spent many hours planning a circle, holding circles, and holding our companions as we navigate ways to bring healing to ourselves and to our world, regardless of how big or small our reach.

While listening to her story in a circle, and now also when we gather as friends who have become sisters, I appreciate Erricka1s willingness to express herself with such conviction, faith, and freedom, especially when she shares the importance of Self-Care. With each new challenge that life continues to bring her way, Erricka dips first into her self-care tool kit, which helps her extend her compassionate reach to soooo many people with whom she connects in her daily travels.

On this day, when I intentionally carved out time to write this foreword, I received two quotes about songs. The first is from Adrienne Maree Brown, who shared, "If I hold jealousy in this life, it's of people who are in lineages that have remembered their songs."

When I had the privilege of reading Erricka's story, I felt no jealousy. I felt shocked, amazed, touched, saddened, frustrated, and awestruck all at once and at different intervals. Offering this foreword helps me reflect on these feelings one at a time.

I felt shocked because I met Erricka after she had endured and fought her way back from depression and hopelessness when accepting herself with humility brought forth joy, encouragement, and love. She has shared how hopeless she had become during our visits; I now understand the courage she conjured to live her way into choices that would carve out her healing path. I am amazed at her perseverance and commitment to herself. Some could argue that "She took so long," and all I receive on these pages is her promise to herself first, which helped her expand her loving care to others. Touched by the presence Erricka brings to all situations, from painfully traumatic to infinitely joyful. Even when flattened by·some experiences, somehow Erricka stays attentive to the deep voice that affirmed her goodness and worth. I am saddened and frustrated that, like Erricka, sometimes life brings so many traumatic events to the same people, which is exacerbated by racism and oppressive systems, forcing breaks and interruptions to people's songs. Lastly, I continue to feel awestruck at my dear friend's willingness to share her story, even though revisiting her journey evoked vulnerability, risk, PTSD, and self-judgment. How incredible that Erricka continues to choose the beauty that comes from a passion for learning, for believing, and for allowing herself the freedom to live her life out loud in truth, love, and faith, inviting you to receive her story in your own chosen way, to do with what you will, when you will. To me, Ericka's journey brings celebration, and even if she lost her song somewhere along the way, she definitely reclaimed it.

The other quote comes from Maya Angelou(sometimes also attributed to Joan Walsh Anglund):

"A bird doesn't sing because it has an answer, it sings because it has a song." Embracing Errickais a brilliant symphony of melodies that grow faintin some places, then resonate in ways that bring tears to our eyes for all its beauty and grace. The songs that stay with me are those that

have harmony and lyrics that bring me a messageof play, hope, love, or awakening; they often have refrains that I belt out over and over, sometimes 10 to 13 times (as long as I am alone!

8, and somehow bringan answer as I sing it) until they somehow find a place into my Self

Care toolbox. Erricka is very clear that this book is not a novel to be read chapter by chapter, and you will find some refrainsin most of her stories. You may read some pieces of Erricka's healing many times. My intuition tells me that each time Erricka shared what we may see as repetition, she actually got to peel away one more layer of her pain and add it to her song. I hope you experience some peeling away of layersof your own; I know I did. And I also pray that Erricka's story helps you find ways to access your own and eventually embrace the beauty that is your song.

Thanks for singing your song, Erricka.It's already reached Platinum Gold for me!

- Amy Vossen Vukelic

MY INTENTION

As you begin to read this book, please note it is a collection of my many emotions that I battled with for years, including while I was depressed and suffering from heartache, amongst other things. It is not meant for you to read this book as a chapter book, reading from cover to cover, chapter to chapter, from the beginning to the end. I purposely wrote it so that you could go directly to the table of contents and locate the chapter title that resonates with you and where you are in your journey in life right now. After you read over the titles of the chapters, you will know exactly where you need to begin your healing journey.

You will also notice that I repeat things in some of the chapters, and that is also done on purpose, for it is needed in this journey of healing our lives. It is how I began my healing. I had to begin and then allow myself to start over again and again, sometimes several times before things would start to work. Doing this without giving or allowing judgment from myself or others as I worked hard to discipline myself to do the things I set out to do while reassuring myself that it is ok to repeat the things that work and keep growing and moving forward on my road to healing my life.

I began writing this book upon noticing how humanity has been so disconnected, and there is so much suffering. Everyone is on their electronic devices first thing in the morning and is no longer connecting to their loved ones. Often, people do not know how to have a conversation. They are afraid to talk. Fear seems to have most people as prisoners, leaving them stuck, not knowing how to have a conversation or how to connect. From the moment we awake, most of us begin our day in fear, anger, upset, mad, and frustration, feeling and thinking we are alone.

I decided to write this book to help heal the lives of people. Who woke up feeling as I had for a very long time. I could not see a way out for many years when I was stuck in a dark place. I was suffering from the traumas of life. I understood that being unhealthy and traumatized had me stuck. When I began reaching out, my healing started, and I realized that when people are healthy, connecting is much easier. Being healthy helps us to humble ourselves. We can then allow ourselves to reach out to help someone else as they struggle to become who they were meant to be and live out their purpose. We watch them grow as they do what makes them happy and full. Understanding you didn't have to be healthy to begin, I began turning my journals into a book.

I hope my words will touch your hearts and souls and place a smile on your face that fills your heart with joy. As my conflicting truths and heartfelt reflections resonate with you and humanity, it is my hope that I help others know they are not alone and we are in this together. We all fail and fall down in life. It is okay; don't stay there; get back up and equip yourself with tools to push your way through. My intent is to empower others to wake up to the reality that we all go through struggles. I believe it is time to come together in love and compassion while embracing our awareness that we all wake up each day with many different feelings, fears, and emotions that often run through our minds, causing us to be stressed and overwhelmed. The truth is that not everyone wakes up happy and ready to begin the day. I know I didn't for many years.

I was always afraid of what might happen. Just thinking about change would put a knot in my stomach to the point that I was almost paralyzed and at the point of throwing up. For some reason, I just wanted time to stand still. I was so afraid that I was not going to be able to handle another thing. I was so overwhelmed whenever I decided to dare to do something different. Choosing to embrace what I was feeling with love, I took three deep breaths and recognized my emotion for what it was. It was terrifying at first. I had to feel it and allow myself to feel the pain and face my fears. As I made a conscious decision to just be in my space, each morning, I began to feel peace.

Believing in myself by releasing negativity in peace and love and choosing to be in charge of my day helped me to take root in where I am in life. Learning to control the beginning of my day helped me handle each challenge that came my way as the day progressed.

When we begin reacting from peace, love, joy, and happiness, then, I believe, humanity will move in a new direction. When we no longer focus on fear when we get up, and instead replace the fear with faith and practice giving love to everyone we meet, I believe the depression rate will drop. Suicide, drug abuse, excessive alcohol usage, and domestic violence will end.

My hope for you reading my book is that families will put down their electronic devices, wait a few minutes, and first connect with each other by choosing to restore and repair the harm that has been done in our lives. My hope is that you recognize that you are not alone. Many of us start the day in a state of fear, but I have learned that we have the power and free will to choose our paths for each day. I believe the God that lives in each one of us heals. I choose to create a better me by giving self-love and self-care to me first and by understanding that my choices are what can make a real difference.

By making the best choice for whatever situation I am dealing with, by thinking better thoughts, and by changing the negatives into positives, as I have learned from my mentors, I am taking steps to create the next chapter in my life.

Embracing Erricka, My Journey From Fear to Faith is meant to encourage the reader and enlighten them that it is perfectly okay to wake up negative. We all do it. We have a choice to let it go. I pray this book will bring hope to God's family through reading these words. My hope is that through healing, people will embrace that no matter where you are in life, you are loved and important for our progress as a community.

I do believe that this book can begin to shift the trajectory of millions of lives as we navigate from fear to faith with choice and love. It's possible if you believe, as I believe, that God's grace is sufficient.

SEPARATION
The thought of separation had my heart in turmoil

When you have your back against the wall, and you are forced to contemplate making the decision to try separation, leaving the one you love and the life you had built together, the emotions are almost indescribable. Instantly, it felt as if my heart was ripped from my chest. Just thinking of the effect it would have on us all was devastating! I know there is no one on this earth who truly wants to make this decision, but how much is enough? I mean, how many promises are you supposed to hear and want to believe before something really bad happens? Every time you go with that empty promise, another drunken event takes place. You know you're grateful that it was just ranting and pounding on walls and swearing. So, in your head, it is not that bad, right? There is no real violence; I would repeat this to myself and then tell myself that everyone loses their cool and gets angry. This didn't happen all the time, so maybe I could handle this and get him to some counseling.

There were many reasons to stay in my marriage; I mean, in my head, we were going to live happily ever after, and everything was worked out. The reality of it all was the reasons to leave were beginning to outweigh the reasons to stay. He had some serious habits that desperately needed to be addressed. I know he loved us and our family, but if I continued ignoring the issues, our livelihood would not survive. He needed to give these issues attention; it was not up to me to try and force it. I would bring it up so much that I felt like I was becoming a nag, and that was not my intention; I wanted to save my marriage. He would tell me I kept repeating myself. I just wanted him to understand the seriousness of it and that I was afraid something bad might happen.

We would have arguments about him staying out all night, he would promise me it was not going to happen again and do something really sweet to make up for it. Things were good the majority of the time, so of course, I would forgive him and not push the issue. It was frustrating, and at times, it was like living life on eggshells. I was furious every weekend, usually Friday night. I was abruptly awakened early Saturday morning by cursing and swearing with loud noise and pounding. When someone is under the influence, you can't trust the words coming out of their mouth or how they will behave. I was getting nervous because my parents divorced, and I feared we would be headed in that direction if things did not improve. My Dad was abusing drugs and alcohol and was abusive to my Mom. It is why they divorced. Domestic violence was what ended their marriage.

I feared if this continued, he might become abusive, and our children might witness something awful or be hurt. The yelling and screaming and staggering around the house, banging into things, was bad enough every time he came home in a drunken rage. I began to fear what could happen. Usually, he was just loud and disruptive, falling to sleep once I calmed him down. He was loud but never physically harmful. All of a sudden, it became more frequent after the birth of our second child, who turned about six months old. He began going out again more frequently. I had begun to become bitter about it. I had grown tired of the weekend partying. It had gone from the weekend and extended to Thursday through Sunday. If I said anything about it, he would stay out longer. Having a few was okay, but when he would overdo it, he would become someone I did not know. If there was a fight at the bar, it stayed with him. He was an angry, drunk, and frustrated when he stumbled in from the bar, but he didn't realize it. Drinking so much at times that he would black out, and only God knows how he made it home alive and safe. I almost hated Friday and Saturday nights. They always started good but never ended well.

The next day, it was as if it never happened. I was out of my mind to even mention the goings-on from the night before. It was as if he wasn't the person who kept me up all night. We would just act as if the event never took place. Well, I thought he would probably feel stupid after realizing what he had put our neighbors and family through the night before. I later realized he was so drunk he blacked out, and he really didn't know what happened; I, on the other hand, remembered every single detail. I would go to sleep tired and upset with him and wake up angry because I knew the week would be wonderful but the weekend would be here before I knew it and the cycle would repeat.

I know if he realized what went on and how he reacted to being heavily intoxicated, he probably would have never wanted to get drunk again. Life was good for years, but something turned. I didn't know what it was, but I did know it was now happening weekly. It was like night and day; sober life was what I craved for him, so our home was peaceful. My nerves were shot and I was talked out because my words were going on deaf ears.

One night, he rolled in, and I let him have it, telling him he needed to grow up and let this party life go. We have a beautiful family now, and he needs to realize it because I did not know how much more I could take. He slammed the door on his way out, yelling, "What the f*** you gonna do?" He left and stayed out until the wee hours of the morning, returning intoxicated, which was no surprise.

I was sitting on the couch with our youngest as he began talking loudly. The other two were in the bedroom sleeping. He said, "Were you threatening to leave me, Erricka?" I didn't say anything to him, and he repeated the question louder, grabbing the phone and throwing it at the wall above my head, scaring us all, screaming that if I did, he would kill me. He stood there, staring at me, screaming over and over, "I will kill you. Do you hear me, Erricka?!" At that moment, I believed he would have.

I thought to myself, Lord Jesus, please protect us all. He was still drunk from the night before and upset about the words we had before he left the house. He knew I meant business because it always took a lot for me to get upset. We got along very well and hardly ever argued, so for me to be mad was important. It was probably weighing on his mind all night. The words he said made me think twice, I never thought I would ever hear my husband speak to me like that. Telling me I would be the next Nicole Simpson if he had anything to do with it. I realized he was serious and not about to let me go willingly. I needed to calm him down by talking to him as I always did. When something was bothering him, I could always reach him when no one else could. We were inseparable and had a strong bond.

I then began reassuring him that everything was okay now, but I was still upset with him for staying out all night. If he wanted everything to be good again, he would have to sleep on the couch, promise not to stay out all night anymore, and keep his word. He agreed and went to the living room with the baby, and I went to our bedroom, first checking on our other two in the bedroom and then grabbing some black garbage bags.

As they took a nap, I was in our bedroom packing my things and shoving them into the back of our large closet so that they wouldn't be noticeable. I was scared, but I knew this was the sign I needed. I had prayed for direction if I should stay or leave. Praying if I leave, if we separate maybe he would get the counseling needed and slow down on drinking and his more than social occasional drug use. I know in our twenties, it is what most people did, but honestly, I was exhausted. I was willing to do whatever was needed for my family and to save our marriage. I did not wish to destroy the life we had made together, but I could not ignore these huge red flags that were right before me. I felt torn and scared because desperation had him talking crazy and psychotic.

Usually, his bark was way bigger than his bite, but could I take that risk, and one of us would be hurt? No, I could not. At times, when he was so intoxicated, it was like I didn't know who he was. It was as if something was literally possessing him, and it was scary. When he was sober, he was awesome. He was a wonderful husband and father so dedicated to our family. It was like night and day, as if he were two totally different people.

What I realized was that I could not just throw all these red flags under the rug, so to speak. This was huge, and it needed to be addressed. We could no longer just keep living this way. I knew I had to act gingerly and not provoke him. Which is what I did and while I was in that bedroom scared and riddled with fear, I made a decision. I was done being worried and scared every single weekend, wondering if something bad might happen when he came home drunk or if he would make it home without hurting himself or someone else drinking and driving. To me, this time, he went overboard with those threats on my life. What would the next time be like? Would I live to tell about it, and what would happen to our children? Realizing he had thrown the telephone over my head, one wrong move and our son or myself could have been badly harmed.

After being startled awake, It took a few moments to calm our other children. Tell them that Daddy is upset, to please stay in the room. I was grateful they were good boys and listened. As the thoughts of what had just taken place ran through my mind, I became enraged myself. Thank God I was locked in our bedroom; it was then that I thought to myself, "How am I going to get out of this nightmare"? I feared for all of our lives in those moments, hours, and days because he was not leaving the house.

While in that room, I thought of the conversations with Mom and what she had gone through being in domestic violence so many years ago. There were still things that had triggered her to this day. Domestic violence caused so many issues throughout life that she had to heal from; it was not easy, and she did not wish it on anyone. Although my husband was not physical, his screaming and yelling scared me stiff where I stood. His yelling and screaming went through me and paralyzed me. I knew if it got to me, what would it do to our babies? Now, he was threatening to take my life because I did not wish to live in this uncertainty. I was trapped in this house with him in fear, waiting for him to go to work so that I could escape this vicious cycle. Thinking of Mom's courage to leave so that we didn't have to suffer gave me the courage to believe I could make it out, too.

I remember her saying you never talk about leaving. It could be the last thing you ever do; just do it. Domestic violence was a tough conversation, but Mom stressed the importance of hard conversations with us growing up. Usually, over dinner, she would talk with us about how our day went and then hit on some life lesson. At the time, being a kid, I thought she was nuts. Still, as time went on, those conversations came in handy. I often remembered and could refer back to them being grateful. Although, at times, the conversation was a bit awkward depending on the subject. When she brought up domestic violence, that was sad. I remember her saying to us hopefully, you will not ever have to be in a domestic violence situation, but at least you are aware of it and that things can turn deadly in seconds. One action can cause him to feel backed into a corner and make him react.

Years later, here I was, and I thought to myself, I want to prevent any harm from taking place. I want to make it out and raise our children. I gave love in those moments when I really wanted to run screaming. I began to fill up those black garbage bags faster with my clothes, pilling them in the back of our closet. I then pulled the hanging clothes to the front so they looked normal, and then I laid down.

I was so scared I had the hammer and the kid's bat under the bed just in case, praying he stayed in the living room. He knocked on the door, and my heart beat quickly. I said through the door that I am still mad at you for staying out all night, remember? You are sleeping on the couch. He said yes and went to the living room. I had come out of the room to get the telephone, and he did not want me to use it. I told him I always talk to Mom and haven't. I need to let her know everything is okay. He told me to make it quick. At that moment, I could not believe what I was hearing, but I said okay. I did not want to make waves. I called Mom, whispering I may need help, but please do not come over or call right now. She said okay, but I know she wasn't happy.

I heard him coming quickly towards our bedroom, so I hurried up and got off the phone. He made dinner, and things calmed down. The next day, he apologized and said how sorry he was for the thought of being without me, and our family drove him nuts just thinking about it. He said I couldn't do it, I would just have to kill you. The thoughts of someone else raising our kids. He looked so sad. I could kinda relate to what he was saying, but there were better ways to deal with it than death. I knew he was serious, so I kept it together. My Grandma always said never let them see you sweat. She would tell me, you can be torn up on the inside, but don't let it show on the outside when we would get into an argument with the kids in the neighborhood. I remained cool as a cucumber.

There is nothing a mother won't do to protect her babies. We played games, and then his oldest son was picked up. I cleaned up after dinner, bathed the boys, and put them to bed. He slept on the couch again. I just was not ready to be that close, yet each day seemed so long. That was the longest week of my life. Every night I kept telling him I wasn't feeling well, so he went to sleep on the couch and took care of our boys. I went to the bedroom, closed the door, continued packing until I was tired, and then went to sleep. Although I knew his bark was way bigger than his bite, he was talking about killing me this time. This was serious and just could not go without some kind of action.

Monday came, and boy, was I happy to see the weekend go, but he was still lying down at 1 pm and not making any attempts to look like a person who was getting ready to go to work. I was preparing his lunch when he came into the kitchen, stating you don't have to do that because I am not going to work. My heart dropped as he stated he was going to be staying home for a few days. This was not planned. He just made this decision, and my insides went crazy. He stayed home all week watching me carefully. It was kind of creepy, but I remained calm and kind. Inside feeling nervous and sick because he threatened to kill me and tried rationalizing it to me. Yet I allowed him back in our bedroom, doing all my wifely duties to reassure him all was well. I'm still a bit nervous about my bags packed in the back of the closet. It was now Friday, and he had finally gotten up and ready for work. Inside I was so nervous because when he kissed me goodbye, saying to me I love you and, remember what I said, I can't lose you. I told him I forgive you, now go to work, I love you.

I knew this was the day it was going to happen. He left for work, and I began to shake. I was filled with so much fear, thinking to myself, was he testing me would he be right back? I was pacing and trying to remain calm as the kids played in their room. After forty-five minutes, I mustered up the strength to call his job and ask the person at the desk so that I knew he was there. Asking them to please not mention I called. He was there, and I said thank you and hung up the phone.

I knew it was the right time to call Mom and ask for help to get out now because he worked from 3 pm to 11 pm and would not be there to fight with me. Fear had taken over, and I couldn't stop shaking when I dialed Mom's number. She picked me up, and I told her everything. I was crying, and she said don't worry, it is going to be okay. She said I am calling to get help. Call your friend with the truck, and we are on the way. I did, and within a half hour, everyone was there. My one sister took the kids with her and Mom, and the rest began gathering my things. They asked what I was taking. I said just the kids' room and my clothing in the back of my closet in those black garbage bags and the washer and dryer because I didn't want to take the kids to the laundromat to do our clothes.

I was thinking I wanted him and the kids to still have a home when they went over for visits with him. I didn't want to hurt him, but I couldn't act like this was not happening. I was scared of my husband after he made those threats. I stood shaking and crying. I couldn't even help them pack me up. It was truly the hardest thing I had ever had to face. I felt torn, scared, angry, betrayed, hurt, and so many other emotions that were rushing through my mind and body at the same moment. My Mom hugged me and said you are safe as they packed the truck. My Uncle said why are you shaking and scared? We are here now, and you don't have to be afraid. I told them I couldn't help it. My body and emotions had taken control, and for a little while, it would not let me stop shaking.

I feared explaining to the boys that we were not going home, grateful they were with my sister for the night. They finished packing me up, and we drove to Mom's upstairs apartment. This would be home for us for a while. I knew he would come look for us when he realized we were gone. Later that night, after he got out of work, he did come yelling, ranting, and raving. Where is my f***ing wife and kids? Screaming all kinds of profanities at Mom telling her he was going to get his gun and if he caught me with someone, it was over for all of us. Mom told him to leave several times. I yelled for him to leave and told him I couldn't come back, but he could have the kids for visits. After a lot of screaming, he finally left when Mom told him she was calling the police because of the gun threats. He came back the next day with the screaming and yelling, threatening what he would do. Every day, he would come by insisting for me to come home. I spoke to him and said we are over. There was no way I could go back unless he quit the drinking and got some counseling. His anger and continued rage made it clear what I was doing was right. If we could not talk without threats and rage, the separation was my only choice at that point. That next week, I think it was a Monday, I went to get an Order of Protection and was given a court date for us to appear. I received my Order Of Protection, and he got supervised visitation and assigned to anger management. While he was in an anger management program, we had counseling for the kids and a few sessions of family counseling.

This was so needed because he constantly broke the rules and stalked me, not abiding by the Order of Protection. Every time I looked up there he was, following me to and from. On the way to drop the kids off to the babysitter on my way to work, he attacked me one time in the middle of the street, dragging me by my hair while I tried protecting our kids, who were right there trying to help me, jumping out of the stroller kicking and biting him so he would let go of me. I had to take the brunt of it because we were in the middle of the street, and I didn't want our children hurt. Thank God Neighbors came to help, and he took off. It was so embarrassing, and it was very tough for a few years. Child Protection Services was called on me several times for various reasons.

He would be on my porch with knives, threatening me. It was like a huge nightmare, not my actual life, but it was and is one of the reasons why we stayed separated and then headed in the direction of divorce. It was the stalking and harassment that landed him in his vacation spot, also known as jail, for months: I had found an apartment down the street from Mom and was so grateful God blessed me with a place of my own but still close to Mom. Though I so appreciated Mom being directly upstairs from her was too close, I needed a little distance between us. It was the first time in my life that I was on my own because I went directly from Mom to living with my ex.

While in jail, he would call and speak to our children, always requesting to speak to me as well. At first, I was very hesitant. I did not wish to hurt him any more than he was already hurting. Being separated had now turned into me planning for a divorce; time had gone on, and I had begun to see someone else. It was hard because I still loved him so much that my heart ached badly. I just wanted the pain to stop, and since it was clear to me, we were over. I said yes to my best guy friend when he asked me out on a date. I knew I could trust him, and he wouldn't break my heart because it was already broken anyway. It was nice to have someone to talk to and do things with when I wasn't crying myself to sleep. He was amazing with the kids and knew they came first, no questions asked, and that I was mad at the world, hurt and broken in every way. He was too, so it was okay. We would be there for one another giving support. It was enough at that moment and worked well. I was learning to be okay with not being in a relationship but it was hard at first and I could not believe this was my new life. I began to try and move on.

One day my husband called for the kids and they told me Dad wants to talk to you Mom. I hesitated at first, but I got on the phone. He asked how I was and said he was thinking of what had happened. He told me he was sorry and knew I had been seeing someone, so he forgave me. After what happened, he was not surprised; he knew he lost me and that I had moved on. He stated that he needed you to know that I still love you and that he wanted our family back. I told him I was glad he was doing well. I wanted nothing but the best for him, but he was like so many of us drifting in life, trying to act like we didn't have issues. I told him we can't do that anymore. I have moved on, assuring him he will always be the kids' Dad. I would not ever allow anyone to take his place with them. He asked me to just think about it, and I hurried off the phone. I thought about it because I wanted it in my heart but was so afraid to return to that life. I tried to put the thought out of my mind, and I did for a bit.

He would write letters to the kids, and one day, he sent a letter to me, too. I opened it, read it, and then I cried putting it in my drawer. He said everything I wanted to hear in that letter, telling me when he got out, he was going to continue his healing, and he wasn't going to drink more than six beers, no more experimental drug use, that stuff wasn't important, our family was all that mattered. He was ready to move past this and didn't wish to waste any more time. It sounded good, and I wanted to believe it. I went on and ignored the letter, acting as if he never sent it. Emotionally distraught but moving through my day to day task. My friend I was dating snuck in my drawer. He had seen where I put it. He read it and then told me that he did read it and that when my ex gets out of jail, I should do what I feel in my heart. He said I know you are thinking about it, and it is tearing you up inside. You will hate yourself if you do nothing. If it is what you want, I will understand, he said I want you and the kids to be happy.

He said he would always be a friend from a distance because he would have to leave town, and he loved me. He was not going to stick around and watch.

He knew me and that I wanted to do everything possible. If I didn't have to divorce, it would be good for the kids; maybe jail changed him. He told me it sounded like he changed the letters anyway. I told him I was sorry, but he was right. I had to try one last time. I felt so bad because I knew he was hurt, but so was I. We spent time together while he planned to leave town. He assured me he would be there if I needed him, and it would be hard, but walking away was what he had to do. I didn't wish to hurt him any more than he already was hurting, so I agreed with him and thanked him.

I then made the decision to give it a go. My ex, also known as my husband, whom I had been separated from for a few years on my way to divorcing, was now writing and calling me and our children. I had finally answered his letter and told him we could do this. He was so happy, and so were all of us. We would talk on the phone every week and write to each other. It felt like the right thing. I was scared to take the risk, but our family was worth it. I thought to myself that if he were for real this time, we would soar because our love was off the charts. Surely, he had chosen us and our family. It would be enough this time.

He got out of jail, and we were reunited as a family. It was beautiful as if we were in a dream. Two and a half months had passed, and it was the "Taste of Buffalo". We first went to the kid's t-ball game and then to the Taste with family and friends. We were there all day enjoying and having a great time. The plastic beer mugs were beginning to pile up, and I felt myself getting irritated. Praying this day was going to end on a good note. The kids began to get cranky because they were tired, I knew it was time to go home. It was now 7 pm, and we had been out all day. I had a couple of wine coolers early when we first arrived but stopped at two, as always. I knew I was the designated driver. Noticing we had about ten plastic mugs and getting upset that he had gone past six. I stated I think we should go home, and that sparked an argument. Him telling me I just don't want him to have any fun.

I had to remind him we had been out here all day and that our children and I were exhausted. Stating we are going home, you can stay or come with. He wasn't happy but came with me, saying he was going out for a bit when we got the kids settled. It didn't matter to me as long as it was peaceful and no drama. I could handle that. For the past few years without him, it has been nice being able to sleep peacefully. Crying myself to sleep was something I had gotten used to. I did not miss being all nervous when he came home drunk. Hoping this time around, he could come home every night, even if he were a little tipsy or drunk, but it tapered off after a bit, and he went to bed without causing trauma to our family. I would be okay with that.

He wanted the keys to drive. I said oh no, let's go. I drove home to my apartment. It was an awkward ride. We got to the apartment and went into the house. Our puppy ran up to greet us, and he drew his foot back and kicked her like a soccer ball across the room, screaming get the heck out of here! She went flying, and all of us were screaming, and that was it for me! I stated it was over and that I was done. It is a good time for you to get your crap and take it to your brothers.

He was yelling at me, are you going to end it over a f**king dog? I stated nope you did after the ten or eleven plastic mugs of beer and then you kicked our puppy!

The kids and I checked on our puppy and I then sent them to the back yard with her, so I could handle things without them around. I told them that if they heard me scream, they should be careful to cross the street and take the puppy to Nana's. They could tell her what happened, and she would know what to do. Daddy would be going away again to get his own house. They went outside, and I told him it wouldn't work and that he had to go that day. This was my apartment, and I was not going to have him disrupt it.

I was biting my tongue all day, trying to enjoy our day with our kids, family, and friends without starting an argument because he didn't keep his word. It took everything out of me, not to mention it, but I didn't. Why? Once again, I gave the benefit of the doubt, believed in my husband, and thought his time away from us was a lesson learned, something he never wanted to go through again. I thought he might drink, but he would do it socially and responsibly and come home to me and our family. There would be no more reason to fear being woken up with pounding, screaming, and yelling, heart beating out of my chest.

I prayed all day at the Taste of Buffalo, asking the lord to show me a sign of which way I should go. Hoping for help for my husband to learn to handle the issues life had dealt him so that he didn't feel like he had to drown his troubles in drinking too much. I realized that drinking was used to celebrate; it was used when he was happy, and when he was sad, it was just something everybody did. I enjoyed it too at times but the overkill, fearing what would happen after made me not like it. Almost every celebration or event was surrounded by alcohol. If he was in a good mood, things went well, but drinking was not a good idea when he was in a bad mood. I knew this would be the first of many events where there would be out-of-control drinking. When we got home and he lost it, so did I. I knew that was my sign; although it was hard and painful, it was what I needed to do.

My separation turned into my divorce there were so many feelings and emotions being expressed throughout my body. I shut them off, and I shut down. I know for so many drinking and partying until you drop arguing, fighting is normal. Some people suffer in silence, acting like this way is okay and dealing with so much pain, but it was not my normal, and I was not going to just go along suffering and allow my kids to make this their normal. He had a right to live his life the way he wanted, and he did not see a problem. It was me, in his eyes, who had the problems. For a while, It got ugly. He would get drunk, stalk my phone, call back to back, call me names, and come to my house banging on my windows, screaming at me; it was awful. I slept with the bat, but now I wasn't afraid. I was now pissed off and tired of his crap.

Opening my curtains to him holding up a large machete knife was embarrassing, and I felt horrible calling the police on my soon-to-be ex-husband, but he gave me no choice. He almost sent me to the crazy house because he would always get away before the police got there. I slipped into depression. I know there are so many who have stayed in these situations, I have no judgments. I know it is hard. There are also many who have not lived to talk about this. I have learned when someone threatens your life, it is a reason to reconsider and take the necessary precautions to keep you and your family safe. I am now grateful to this day for my decision to leave and to divorce. I am not perfect, and I do not pretend to be. I truly had every intention of enjoying my marriage and our life together. The violent rages and the threats on my life had me feeling uncertain. We were two people who saw things differently when it came to having fun after we had children, and also it seemed after about eighteen months, we were also choosing different paths. I know now why he lied to me about his social habits. It was because he knew if he told me the truth, I was not going to stay. After all, it wasn't me.

We all have a right to live this life exactly how we want to, and as we do that, it should not cause the people we love any harm or discomfort. In my heart, I know he loved me, but his habits prevented him from thinking clearly. It was not up to me to tell him what to do and how to do it, I did everything I could and went for outside help as well. We grew up in different households, and what happens in our home as children is normal to us. We then grow up and we create and allow that behavior in our homes or choose to be so far from what we grew up with. My home was peaceful and safe. What I knew and was used to, and when my ex-husband disrupted, it was hard. I would not live the rest of my life in this chaos every weekend. I know we grew up different and to him this was his normal. I had to embrace it for what it was, and I filed the divorce papers and went on with the supervised visitation for some years.

Thinking back now on what happened when we separated, I know we were young and, at times, behaved badly and should have stayed in counseling to heal. He really did want me dead and would have done it if he had not gone to jail. I am no longer resentful or angry, and I forgive him for his actions. I also realized many things factored into his behavior. I had my beautiful mother to whom I could talk on a regular basis. She was an amazing example and mentor. She was always just a phone call away. If he had still had his mother, I know his life would have been so different. He would have had much healthier habits and would have handled life from a place of peace. His actions were coming from a place of fear, anger, and rage. That is not who he was, or the man I married, it was how he behaved when he got drunk, from not dealing with his traumas of life. I did not fall in love with a madman. I fell in love with him, the sober, loving man. Who had dreams of taking on the world and enjoying it with our families?

We created beautiful children from our love, and I know he loves them with everything that he is. He may have been angry at me for separating from him, but if I called him, he would answer, and he would do whatever he could for me. It took years for him to turn himself around, and there were many occasions with him where I just had to hang up the phone because the words he spoke were, in my words," SPECIAL," so I just kept my distance. Healing comes in many forms, and I knew it would take years, but I am grateful he has been blessed with an amazing partner who loves him and our children. My children tell me Dad has had relationships in which he could have been better. This one he is in now is the best he has ever been after us. I am grateful for her and everyone who gives him love and God's grace for him and his relationship.

It is time to heal and break the generational cycles of the past. Every day is a good day to begin again. My separation was the beginning of me separating myself from behaviors I did not like and from domestic violence. I learned that words and behaviors are also harmful and are a part of domestic violence. They can turn into something worse if we don't take the steps to heal all parties involved. We are all important in our relationships, and if we are not healthy when we begin them, we must separate ourselves and get the help we need to become healthy. No one person is more important than the other. If I want my relationships to thrive, it starts with me. I am grateful for my ex and all my relationships; each one has helped me grow.

Separation is not a bad thing in life. I believe we must allow ourselves to separate from the things and people who have harmed us so we can heal and become our best selves. I am a forever learner and healer of my life. I am grateful my separation has brought wholeness into my life and my family. I am opening up and being vulnerable because I want to break these generational cycles of alcoholism and domestic violence of any kind. Healing the lives of my loved ones and anyone who is suffering from this, feeling as if they are stuck and not sure what to do. I don't want to hurt my ex-husband as I open up and become vulnerable about what took place and made me separate from him. I want to share my story and bring awareness. He is the father of our awesome children, and he is human and, like the rest of us, a victim of this world that can be so cruel at times. The world makes it seem okay to live like nothing is wrong and pretend to be a happy family when the truth is trauma is taking place in so many homes.

I hope that healing can also take place in other lives and that separation and divorce will not have to be the answer. After my separation, I began dating, which was weird at first, but I am grateful to my ex-husband because of him. I was no longer that naive; believe anything you say, woman. I had to grow up, and I was not going to allow any other man to come into my home and traumatize us. I learned there are a lot of hurting people who need to heal from their childhood trauma. I am not trying to hurt my ex-husband or anyone else. I realized after separating that his drunken blackouts were why he could get up the next day as if nothing happened. The blackouts caused him not to remember his behavior. He is not the same person he was back then. I know the horrible things he did that he remembers he would like to forget. I also believe when the things he did flashed before him, I am sure he did whatever he could to forget the pain he caused or the pain done to him in the past. I now understand these things probably happened because, at that time, he was not facing his demons.

I believe carrying the pain from the past is why so many relationships today are suffering and why we have so many people who have an addiction or two. I believe it is the time to heal from our trauma. Time to stop pointing fingers at others for being addicted and running from their pain and look in our own mirror. Just because yours is not mine does not mean that you don't have an issue, a problem that desperately needs attention. You can be the one to break the cycle, and every generation can be better. You can turn the page and step into your new life. I now believe separating ourselves from the things that caused us pain begins our healing. I had to realize I was not what happened to me. That was a traumatic experience, and I had the power to stay in it or leave it behind me. I could move forward and embrace what is on my way to healing.

When I did all that I could, I let go and allowed God to work it out however it needed to be worked out. Heartbroken but alive, able to raise my children and mend my broken heart. Utilizing the tools I learned along my healing journey from my mentors to navigate my way through this life that can be hell at times. Each of us has to go through trial and era to find what works for us. What works for me may not work for you, but hearing my story may spark something in you. Maybe you will read this book and see that it is possible to heal your life and create a life in which you can be happy. Think about the word separation and what it means to you, and then take action. Separate yourself from your situation and begin to heal. Realize it is okay to be with yourself, not being in a relationship is okay. Get to know who you are and then live your greatest life.

FAMILY

Our family is simply who we love.

We all want to feel that powerful connection of family ties. It gives us the feeling of belonging, the sense of fitting in somewhere. It is what makes life worth living. When we have a family, we have a place in the world. Knowing there is someone who will be that ear, to listen and voice to encourage you not to give up. We all want the kind of family that will catch you like an airbag when you have fallen, giving you unconditional love and making it easier to get back up and keep moving forward. Most of us want that family that is in our corner, whether we are winning or losing.

Family comes in many different arrangements. It can be biological or blended, with parents or a single mother or father with children. We form families at school, work, the gym, and the many different organizations that we belong to. Our family is truly what we make it out to be. We must put in the time and build quality relationships if we want to have a good life and a strong connection. By understanding that we get what we give, I now realize that in my own family, there were times when I lacked love for myself, and, as a result, I was unable to give love to my family in a way they needed.

In these times, I failed to do my part and received results that I did not like. It was because I had checked out of life and did not know how to handle the pain and heartache I was dealing with. I never saw this part of life coming, it hit me like a ton of bricks. It was my family, all the people who loved me, who were encouraging me to be courageous enough to keep getting up after my many falls and failures. I will forever work on my continuous struggle to be just a little bit better tomorrow than I was yesterday.

I realize that the hugs from various members of my work family got me through some of the toughest times. At the time, there were a tremendous number of life challenges, but somehow, I have had more than the average person. LOL (laugh out loud). My work family, whom I spend more time with than my biological family, is the family I have grown to love dearly. I am grateful for our strong bond. They are with me eight hours a day through good, bad, and ugly trials.

We have one another's back and help maintain our composure during the tough times, which are inevitable. When we lose our crap, and we do, we lift each other with a hug and a smile, like healthy families do.

I believe the universe is one big family that keeps on growing and evolving, getting better. I think the more love we give to one another, the more our family will prosper in magnificent ways allowing each generation to be better than the one before it. We're breaking cycles, baby.

Being present takes work. When you are present, you are in that moment; you are not distracted by the phone, TV, music, or other outside sources. You are giving full attention to the person you are with, even when that person is yourself.

What do I mean, by being present with myself? It is to connect with my breathing, being okay with myself, and loving the skin I am in. It is breathing in the positive, exhaling the negative, embracing the good, and letting go of what I cannot control.

Being present with others, as we continue to pass the love down and correct the huge cyclical mistakes that have been made in our families, I know our world will heal one person, one family, one community, at a time if we can understand that our paradigm has already shaped us and that we do things from habit. Now, it is up to us to change our old habits and create new ones without blame or shame.

I pray more people will begin to take a stand whenever there is an opportunity to be the change by supporting each person in each family in growing into their greater self.

I am grateful I am now choosing to love myself, my family, friends, and loved ones with all my heart. By listening more and judging less, as I have learned from Stephen Richards Covey's The 7 Habits of Highly Effective People, my eyes were opened in many ways. The book blessed me with things to work on in all areas of my life.

Assisting me in growing and becoming a well-rounded person, I found the book to be one of the starting points in my journey to faith. I then began blessing my family with love in more ways than I could have imagined. Now, trusting that they will be drawn to me like moths to a flame whenever they see, hear, or think about me. Their hearts, minds, and souls will be overwhelmed with so much love and joy from the thought of hearing my name that they allow themselves to stop and think for a moment, "I am so loved."

We are one family I do believe. God's family. None of us are meant to be here feeling alone going through this journey. We are all connected by the spirit of God, which lives in every one of us. Giving love to our world one person at a time is truly how we will heal our family, God's family.

PARENTING
It is a skill that must be taught.

Good, bad, and indifferent parenting skills are taught and passed down from generation to generation. Parenting is a huge responsibility. I did not want to mess up, and when I did, it hurt like hell. In reflection, I have realized that our mistakes are how we learn and grow.

After I separated from my ex-husband the pressure was on. It was terrifying at times knowing that I was the sole person to make the decisions for the innocent lives of our children. It was so overwhelming just thinking about what could happen that I often worried and visualized all kinds of craziness. I was overthinking, overreacting, and at times, shutting down instead of being present, being part of the process.

I have learned through experience that we do what we are taught, and sometimes what was taught is not healthy. Generally, if an unhealthy person taught it, unconsciously, we repeat learned unhealthy habits. We then participate in relationships, not realizing they are doomed from the start. People who grow up following the pattern usually do not mean to do this, but it happens. It doesn't make me a bad person. We must learn that if you do not have it, you cannot give it, so without love, there is no possible way for you to thrive being the parent you want or need to be. I believe that getting in touch with the spirit of the God that lives within is the only way to a healthier you, resulting in a healthier family. Again, we are breaking cycles, baby.

Understanding that to be the best parent to our children, we must recognize that it is not about you anymore once that child is born. Our job is to be the very best role model and teacher to our children and all the children we encounter. We are all responsible for shaping and mentoring all children.

The light came on when I witnessed my children playing and repeating one of my bad habits. One night, I was watching my sons play, as kids do, and I saw them acting as if they were drunk as they went to bed to sleep. Seeing them recreate my nightly routine of drinking just a bit too much, I realized in that moment, that what I was doing was not healthy. I was hiding my pain behind the two nightly malt liquors, numbing me so I could sleep. It was the very thing that led to the destruction of my marriage. I was so angry with my ex-husband for choosing alcohol over us, I fell into the trap of alcohol, the same trap that entangled him, to escape the pain. I was afraid of having my children grow up to repeat these bad habits later in life and be hurt by following my teaching. I realized I was a hypocrite and needed to make some changes immediately.

Before the changes began taking hold within me, I found myself being angry at other parents for staying in varying degrees of addiction and abuse. I felt alone and overwhelmed with so much pain. The incident with my sons forced me to remember why I decided to remove us from our family home. It was the exposure of being scared out of our sleep every weekend as he stumbled in, usually ranting and raving about whatever went on at the bar or wherever the drinking fest took place. I was tired of being afraid of what might happen with the man I loved, who seemed to disappear every time he left the house. I had to focus on myself and learn what that looked like, and leaving where I was had to be the beginning of my healing.

While I worked on changing, growing, and embracing myself, I was a work in progress. While I took a step in the right direction, I realize, looking back, I didn't know how to do things differently. Thinking I could escape it, and I did for years, I then, feeling lonely, fell into the trap of another unhealthy partner years later, with a different addiction, due to the traumas of life.

It was not until I began to give love to myself. That it hit me like a ton of bricks landing on me. There are a lot of unhealthy people in relationships raising unhealthy children. I can run from this, but it is everywhere. I realized I must become healthy so I can see and think clearly. Then, and only then, can I have a healthy relationship. I now see the red flags and can make healthy decisions. I do not have to settle for unhealthy behaviors anymore. It starts with me. I now believe I can be the best parent to my children, and a healthy partner in my relationship. My children have always been the most important focus, not always in the healthiest way, but now it is.

My ex-husband is a wonderful man who also loves our children. When he was not drunk, he always went above and beyond as a parent to our sons. I am grateful for all our love in creating our amazing family. For years, I was very angry with him, and I was hurt - alcohol stole our marriage.

I believe this (alcoholism and drug use) lives in the paradigms of my children, nieces, nephews, and others, causing them harm as they put Band-Aids on their pain in some of their adult relationships. I don't wish this on anyone. I truly believe without our addictions we can be our best. It is possible we can learn to heal from them and be a healthy role model. I have learned that our job as parents is also to learn how to deal with the issues of our lives in positive ways.

So, how did I turn my thinking around? Prayer, meditation and my mentors helped me to turn things around. I got to a place where I found myself encouraging my life partner to realize he also had to work on loving himself or there was no way we could go on together. Grateful, he began his journey to a healthy way of living. It was what saved our relationship and made it possible for us to get married.

As I began to give love to myself, I realized that for things to get better, things have to change. I had to become the change and go forward.

Parenting is not easy; it is the hardest but most fulfilling job I have ever had. I will forever be a learner at it. I am so grateful for my gorgeous, bright, amazing young adults, who all bring something wonderful to my life and our world. I have learned as we parent our children, we need all the help we can get. I believe we need to be as healthy as possible to create a more positive world. It is true that raising children takes a village and a community.

BETRAYED
Betrayal comes in many different forms.

Betrayal comes in many different forms. It comes from someone you choose to reach out to so they will know unconditional love in their lifetime. You hope they will see your sincerity and be grateful for the bond you have made with them. The bond comes in the form of a smile, on the face of someone who says I love you. The betrayal is when they willingly do something they know will hurt you.

Betrayal also comes from your child, who may tell a lie about you, not realizing the pain of what they said will have hurt you. One day, after I left his father, my then 3-year-old son fell and busted his lip. That day, he went on his scheduled weekend visit with his dad. Seeing his lip, his dad immediately reacted and yelled, "Your mom did that?" Our young son was afraid and did not respond, so his father called the police, and CPS came to my house to investigate me and check that all was well. While unintentional, and knowing he was just a little boy, the lack of understanding of what was happening ate at me and hurt me in indescribable ways. To this day, my heart breaks for my son; for all of us, his dad was just being a loving Dad, but I do not understand how a man who knew me to my soul could think I would ever hurt our child. However, I do know he was reacting out of the pain of our separation and reacted the only way he knew how.

When children repeat something, they hear something said about you from someone they trust, someone who is present in their life, or from your closest friend who you laugh, joke, and play with; they may not understand that it is not true or the seriousness of the comment. They do not realize how, repeating it to you or, worse, to others, how hurtful it can be. When the one who knows some of your secrets and some of the precious heart-to-heart details of special earth-shaking moments and events in your life betrays you to your child, the pain of betrayal is indescribable.

Betrayal comes from the one calling themselves your best friend as they break your heart, trying to date the man you love behind your back.

Betrayal comes when the guy you begin to date, after years of being alone and dealing with your separation from your soon-to-be ex-husband, steals your rent money out of your purse and lies to you about it. He knows you are a single mother trying to make ends meet, struggling to keep it together, and he pretends to be honest. Then he betrays you again, as he goes along thinking you are blind to the fact he tried to get with your sister. Thank God, your sister did not fall for his trap and had the courage to tell you so you could open your eyes and dump him.

Betrayal comes from an aunt telling you there will be no get-together and that it will be another time. Then you come to find out that there was a celebration there, but you were not invited. For whatever reason, it still hurts and is a betrayal of the heart.

Betrayal also comes from your husband or loved one, who promises you he will not drink again or do that drug of choice which has him under its spell as he stays out all night doing it. I felt betrayed and hurt because drinking and partying seemed to be the most important thing. It had become the other woman, so to speak. Each empty promise after empty promise began to get old, and I got angrier each time. I cried myself to sleep night after night, not knowing how or when this hurt would end.

It is one thing when you are single and dating, but after you marry and have the one you love and a beautiful family at home waiting for you, I couldn't understand how it was okay to do the same things night after night. I just could not see how he could be okay with having me up all night stressed, worried about him, and wondering if he would be safe getting home.

Feeling I was betrayed again as he went out after work, spending the rent money and partying with some of my girlfriends who happened to be at the same bar. One of them betrayed me by getting a little closer to my husband than was necessary. I was told by my best friend, who was on fire and ready to kill the people who were hurting me. Not really kill, but she was feeling my pain while I was devastated, at home, pregnant with baby number two.

To some, it may seem like a whole lot of little things, but to me, it felt astronomical at that time, damaging to both my heart and my soul. This was not meant to cause me pain, but it did. It was just supposed to be a couple of drinks after work. To a pregnant woman with emotions, it was a betrayal. I was doubtful I would ever be able to forgive. Powerfully my mother has always been the voice of reason. She helped me to acknowledge that though each betrayal was painful, the battle was not mine. It is the Lord's. Our heavenly father will deal with it and with those who caused it. Leaving it all in God's hands gave me peace. He would take care of my pain, and I didn't have to do one thing except forgive and let go. Learning to stop being angry and feeling betrayed is not easy. Still, it is a necessary step in growth and in breaking cycles.

SHAME
Tired of waking up feeling shame and humiliation.

There should be nothing that humiliates us, no shameful occurrence that makes us feel pain throughout this life journey. In other words, I feel no challenge or experience has taken place that gives others the right to point a shameful finger at another, including ourselves. Yet, we allow people to think they have the right to punish us for life for a mistake we made in the past. We do something to hurt someone out of anger, and we hold on to the guilt, feeling shame for the pain we have caused by lashing out at our loved ones.

Keeping ourselves in a pain prison, walking around, suppressing the hurt that was done to us while holding ourselves in bondage, we try to do our mundane daily rituals. We stumble from one thing to another, numb, and forbidding ourselves to give or receive love, afraid of risking our hearts. We are ashamed of the person we have allowed ourselves to become. We give up our self-dignity, feeling the guilt, allowing the one we hurt to control us, using guilt and shame as the weapon to keep us right where they want us.

Our shame paralyzes us in the safety zone. Standing still, numb to the world around us, we do not understand that inside, we are dying because we refuse to allow what is. Being afraid to move from our shame we run and hide.

I was embarrassed and filled with shame when I divorced the love of my life. I felt like a failure, though I was the one who left because I was heartbroken that he could not see through the drugs and alcohol that I was there for him, for us, for our family.

As I was checking off the boxes of my wifely, and maternal "duties", I desperately wanted him to do the same for us. When I left, I knew I did the right thing for our children and myself, but it still hurt, a pain that tore me apart. As much as I knew that I had to find my way, it didn't make me feel any better or less guilty. Then, being a single mother, the shame was amplified. I didn't want my kids to grow up without a dad.

The world can be very cruel at times, making it tough, especially for women, to even want to try to break free and strive for better. In fact, we are often our own worst critics. We have all done something that brought us shame at one time or another.

Finding your mistake and facing the consequences is the best way I have learned to move on. Taking the lesson from it was the only way I could hold my head up again. I'm praying I got it, so I never have to repeat feeling shame again.

Freeing myself allowed room for my blessings to flow in, giving me a reason to know and believe that I am worthy, and, yes, I deserve to have a healthy, kind, loving, God-fearing partner. He is not religious, but he is a believer. I believe some religious people are mean, judgmental, and out to cause pain and separation. I needed a partner who believes in God and is ready to grow in faith with me.

WHEN STRUGGLES COME
Life often hits us in the gut, knocking the wind out of us.

Life had hit me on the blindside right in my gut. Paralyzed, I found myself in the same spot for seven years. I had allowed the pain to make me stagnant. It seemed as if it was one struggle after another when suddenly I would be hit with something bigger than what I was already going through; life was hard. I had no intention of moving anywhere. I had allowed myself to become comfortable right where I was at. My only life goal at the time was to stop the pain. Often, it hurt so bad that my stomach was filled with nervousness to the point it made me throw up; I was drowning in fear. Rarely did I want to do anything, fear and pain paralyzed me.

I thank God for my family and friends who would not give up on me. They kept trying to get me moving until they broke me down, and I would agree to join them in attending some event. Being around people was tough, it forced me to try and find a way to hold it together. Let me tell you, it did not always work. It was especially difficult if the kids were not with me. I guess it was pure desperation to feel better that inspired me to try again at life. Let me be clear, there is no designated time to wallow in our misery.

We cannot grow and cannot move on until we are ready. Nothing indeed changes until you get sick and tired of being sick and tired. You must force yourself to do something new by making up your mind and telling yourself that anything is better than what is happening. It was not until I began to listen to motivational videos that I learned that we are not supposed to lie down and take it when life hits us. Mom tried to teach us that as we grew up, but when you're hurting, it is like you must lose all your faculties or something; nothing makes sense. I had to learn to pray again and to pray harder, believe stronger, and trust in my faith that it is already done. I had to learn to "Let go and let God," and to do this, I had to forgive!

Only then could I begin to focus and begin rising to a new level. No longer struggling with what once had me paralyzed and recognizing it is ok to release that mountain of pain because it has run its course, I realized that it is now time for me to receive the lesson in peace and love. I had to realize that struggles are not meant to last forever, to embrace them for what they are and get back up and going at it in a new way this time. Once you understand this, you will realize how much power and strength you have and begin to move your mountains; we are powerful.

Powerful – meaning full of power, a mindset we need to get back up fighting. As you move forward you continue acquiring new skills that will assist you in making life the way you want it. It begins by figuring out what tools work for you, remembering that healing and growth are not a one-size-fits-all remedy. It takes practice, and trial and error. As you figure out what works for you, and you begin to utilize those tools daily, they will begin to propel you to your best life.

By doing the work I learned that each struggle is a level of life that teaches us something we did not know but that we need to go to the next step. I now believe our struggles bring us the knowledge that will help us make better decisions and to help others. We grow if we are willing to receive the lessons, even those seemingly unbearably painful. Pain is wisdom and growth. That painful struggle we are tussling with is honestly here to help you grow, allowing you to see you are ready to do something new.

When I found the strength to leave my then-husband, I realized I was exhausted, and something had to change—and that something was me. Miraculously, I decided to start my day with faith instead of fear, utilizing meditation and prayer, taught by Mom. Once I changed my mindset, my life changed. No longer was I struggling to do anything. I learned to look at the challenge, take a breath, and decide if and what I had to do. Life is good!

ANGER

Trying to receive something good
when you are filled with anger

I went on for several years, waking up angry with nothing nice to say. I realized from the conversations that were taking place at work, the grocery store, shopping center, doctor's office, etc., that I was not alone. In fact, there are so many people just like me. I had to wonder when and if my ship was going to ever come in. It just seemed like one bad thing after another was happening in my life for a while. I had good reasons for feeling angry.

My heart was broken because I lost the love of my life.

The man I had planned on living out my life dreams with, growing old together, and having babies with. Yes, we had the babies, but we were now a broken family. I will admit that before we were married, I did not see the red flags for his party lifestyle. I was blinded by love. After our first son was born, I started to see the red flags, but, again, blinded by love, I convinced myself it would get better, that he would choose us over the drugs, alcohol, and party lifestyle.

The birth of our second son, only 18 months later, showed me that he was not going to change. I was downright angry, pissed off, mad at the world. This is not what I signed up for when I said "I do." Life was bad for me at that time. I was in a very dark place. I realized that being steeped in pain was causing me to make angry decisions. The challenges were not going to last forever. At the time, it hurt like hell and felt like a lifetime of pain. I recognized after I had left, it was me, reliving the pain that fueled me, helping me to stay angry. I was constantly going over and over every conversation, every disappointment, and every broken promise and crying myself to sleep every night.

This was keeping me in my mess. I had to move away from the toxic individuals and stop being toxic to myself and those whom I love. Then I decided to stop waking up every day, jumping up out of bed, and running around like a chicken with my head cut off. I felt a whole new level of anger because he and I were arrested, falsely accused, and humiliated. {See the chapter Believe for details}.

Angry, I began dating and had an emotionless relationship on and off for years. I was afraid to risk giving my heart again. I was struggling with the pain and humiliation of what happened the first time I gave my heart. I was angry because, after years of not allowing myself to feel I had secretly begun to fall in love, I didn't feel that it would be reciprocated. I felt stuck and knew I must do something to change how I felt and lived. I was scared, but I knew it was time. I had to release and let go of the anger. I needed to find a way to feel good again by doing something positive and trying something new.

At first, it was like pretending. To be honest, it was as if I was playing a role in a movie. I was an actress in my own life. So, I made a choice: no longer would I allow anger to rule. I had to decide to stop using negative words and start using only positive ones.

It took a while and a lot of practice, but it began to come more naturally. It was only when I forgave myself for holding on to the pain for so long that I really felt as if I could breathe. Anger does not run my life anymore. I may not wake up happy every day, but when I am done with my daily morning routine, I command my day from the start. I promise I will be happy, joyful, and grateful, ready to celebrate and begin the gift of a new day.

LIFE AND DEATH

Our words have power; we should give love when we speak.

Life and death are in the power of the tongue, so it tells us in what I believe is the greatest book ever written, The Bible, filled with life and death encounters, showing us many different experiences, both good and bad, to learn from. It allows us to see that no one is perfect, not even in biblical times. We wake up each day to a new experience, giving life or death to everything we approach. I have learned the hard way that when you are speaking negative words, you are bringing death into your situation. This negative talk can cause misfortune.

I believe that if you choose to be kind and give love it makes whatever you are working on a bit easier to manage. Perceiving this helped me realize it was time to do a new thing. By trying to be positive and think before I spoke and utilizing kind words before opening my mouth was a bit of a struggle. Giving life to everyone and everything was not always easy. I would sometimes wake up stressed and stuck in fear. I was afraid of how I was going to pay my rent, feed my children, and maintain my household. I was also afraid to say what I was experiencing to anyone because I was not outward with my emotions and did not want to impose what I was going through on anyone I loved.

I would hold all my stuff in. My stomach would be in an uproar, and inside, I would be screaming. Yet, outside, it would appear to others that all was well. I had not given any thought to the words I was speaking, but I now know for sure that my words took part in why my life was at a standstill. I was not feeling good at all. I was constantly feeling like I was dying, waking up crying, going to sleep crying, and pretending life was beautiful while really feeling alone. I had to change my conversation, and I began to monitor my big mouth. What a task that has been.

This was truly the beginning of a new way of life for me. I began to feel better, and life as I once saw it was now a thing of the past. I had begun to progress and grow just from the beginning to monitor the words flowing out of my mouth. No longer was I spouting out death with my negative, angry words and conversations. I had decided to choose life. Now, this did not blow up overnight, in fact, it took me years to get this under some sort of control. I immediately noticed that things started getting better as I started to give more love to myself and my surroundings. I began to let the sun in.

The better I began to feel, the lighter I felt, and it became easier to give love to my life. Waking up started to feel good. The happier I became the better choices I began to make. I started listening to positive affirmations and audiobooks. No more was I talking negatively about myself or others, no good can come from that anyway. Doing that caused me to feel horrible, and I did not like the person I was developing into with the negativity. My new tools of positivity and self-awareness were now a habit. This made it much easier for me to choose to release that old habit of speaking negatively and ultimately creating a sort of inner death.

Now, I am happily giving life and love to everything and everyone I meet. I read inspirational books and listened to Oprah Winfrey's life classes on Own Network. They were enlightening and helped me heal and connect spiritually. Having a good pastor (Jerimiah Carter at Bethel Tabernacle) and supportive family and friends was, and is, the cherry on top for me. I absolutely love and adore my family.

WEIGHT OF LIFE
The layers we carry on our bodies are
the weight life has dealt us.

Being swamped with everyday life as a single mother and feeling devastated after my divorce became my life. I just could not believe that our love could ever be separated. Our love was magical, filled with bliss, joy, and laughter, and we were so connected that every day together was like walking on air. I felt so loved, and we worked well together for a long time. I now believe this is why it took me so long to bounce back. It was truly a struggle to do the things needed to keep life flowing. I had begun to procrastinate; I put on weight, and never saw it coming.

I was carrying the weight of life all over my body and feeling very heavy. Many days it seemed as if I just could not get a break. Being a single mom is a blessing and 24 hour-7 days a week job. It was getting tougher to get up. There were days I felt weak, drained, and very alone. I pretended to be happy, but inside, I was dying and crying. I wouldn't wish this astronomical pain on my worst enemy. My heart had a surplus of pain in it. Heartbroken and financially broke was a tough place to be, it was hard.

Dealing with the hardships of life is one thing when you have a partner to help you, but when you are facing it alone, it feels insurmountable. When it is you who must make it happen for your life and others who depend on you, those mountains become heavy weights. After about seven years of carrying this endless weight of immense pain I was ready to do life, scared, but finally ready for something else. I did not want this weight on my children. They were growing and very smart. I couldn't hide from my fears forever. How would I transform from this dark place I had been living in? It was not until I began to be grateful for what I have that I finally started thinking that no matter what obstacles were thrown at me, I had amazing children, family, and friends and could handle and overcome my challenges.

Then, I began disciplining myself by creating a daily routine. After listening to my mentors from audiobooks and reading personal development books, I began to perceive a smidgen of hope. My daily routine empowered me to handle the weight that life had given me. I allowed myself to first recognize my part in getting where I was in life. I had also made choices that took me off course, but it wasn't too late. By learning to confront my issues one by one and understanding that the weight I am carrying will not last forever, I can change the trajectory of my family's life.

If I begin to focus on looking in my mirror and then eagerly begin to take solid positive steps, I could no longer hold on to my old, negative habits of being angry. I learned to embrace and allow what is, then release and let them go. I began to feel empowered because I decided to release the weight of life. By forgiving myself first, I then decided to commit to myself and started being accountable for the direction my life would go in. I began handling one weight at a time, learning the lesson of each one so that I could be better today than yesterday.

I began dedicating myself to watching, reading, and listening to audiobooks on personal development and motivators from some of the greatest life teachers. I didn't believe doing this stuff would work at first. I was trying it because I had nothing to lose. I am so grateful for every motivational and personal development teacher. They helped me to come alive again when I began to act out and then practice some of the teachings I had been learning. I became that positive person I had dreamed about and lived a different experience. I was enjoying life for the first time in years. It is true that God's grace is sufficient. When you release the weight of life and let go, let God handle it.

LETTING GO
Freeing ourselves from the prison we have made

We are all attached to our material things. We love them like we love our family members. Most of us hold on to our things and relationships much longer than we should. We usually outgrow them but do not release them when we need to. I have learned that our gut tells us the relationship is over. You feel it and refuse to let go and stay in it, bitter and afraid to release it and allow yourself to move forward. Being angry at our partner when we should be angry at ourselves for not doing what we know is needed makes us bitter and angry.

We know that letting go in peace and love is the right thing to do. When we allow what needs to take place to happen naturally, the pain settles, and we can allow ourselves to receive the blessing. The problem is, most of us don't do that, we fight it. It took me years to see I was in my own way. It was me blocking my goods from coming to me. As I held on to the things of the past, filled with bitterness, hoping he would change. When I knew I needed to just go on and get that divorce, I was then forced to learn the very harsh lesson of how to live life as a single mom. We can't change anyone but ourselves and make them do what they are not ready to do on their own. I had to forgive him and let go.

Another example of learning to let go was when my sister, who had been ill for a long time, passed. We had just had an incredible, happy, and loving visit. It was also the day she left us. I was convinced she would be coming home, little did I know that she did go home, just not the earthly one. Holding on to my sister when she was dying, not wanting to let her go when she was ready, I was holding on to the impossible. She was so happy to be free from this earth and gave me the gift of seeing her shine. It was so peaceful that day, and I could actually see the light in her. I just never thought that would be the last time I would be with her. She passed that night after I left, and I was stunned; it couldn't be true. Looking back, I realize, at times, it is very difficult for us to allow those we love to move on and be in peace. We hold on to them based on our needs. I realize now that it is not about me; it is about doing what gives them peace, even if we do not approve. I now understand that it is not always about how I feel when it comes to my loved ones.

I had a wall of protection built up. There was no other way of doing things. I had myself in a box of negativity and pain, not understanding that accepting and releasing pain would free me from the space I desperately wanted to be free of. I had to remember the tools Mom taught us as children: practice gratitude and meditation, let go, and let God guide me, and only then would I be free of the weight of the heaviness of the challenges of life.

LOSS
It is not a bad thing. It is understanding

Coming to grips with the fact that loss happens and it is a part of life is not an easy thing to accept. It is the truth that we are born to die, and staying alive and healthy is a task at times. Every time we learn something new, that old thinking now is a thing of the past. The new thing becomes our new knowledge. It is truly up to us to receive it and hopefully teach it to the next generation in peace and love. I do now understand that we are here to bring love and help evolve, even when we have experienced loss.

I have come to see that we rise only if we apply our new knowledge. So, it is not a bad thing to let go of someone or something that is causing us pain or suffering. We usually feel pain because we love them hard, giving our whole selves to everything we choose to commit to. In my own experience, I have found that letting go is truly easier said than done. I believe that everyone I have been blessed with in my life comes with a gift for me to learn, even the ones I lose. I began to see that everyone I lost taught me a lesson, and now I am more open to receiving.

My wish is that, hopefully, by reading my book, others can learn and grow from my lessons, and we can pass forward a new way of healing and teaching others as we go on throughout our lives, sparing them a little heartache. Like everything in life, it is a process we must learn to believe in while trusting in God to get us through. When I lost my sister, I thought it was the end of the world. My heart was ripped wide open. There is truly nothing as special as the bond you share with your sister. I don't believe you can ever replace such love.

Looking back at that moment, I see that she was teaching me to embrace life when she told me she was going home. It was the very last day we spent together. She said it three times, "I am going home." As she grabbed my face and looked me in the eyes, I said, "I know." Then she said it again, saying, "Baby, I am going home. You must teach our brothers, sisters, and children to love God with all their hearts. Tell them to pray about everything. I laughed and said, "Yeah, and you need to help me do this, Reese." (That was her nickname.) She ignored what I said and went "Home" to God. She knew what I could not accept because she embraced the Spirit that was in her; I was too busy with the pain and grief to see that she was truly happy; she was leaving her life of pain and embracing the light she was with God.

That same day, she stated, "Little Herb needs help with that baby." Our brother was having a baby with his long-term girlfriend. It never dawned on me that she was telling me that she knew it was her time to leave this earth plane and that I had to help Herb without her.

That day was one of the happiest moments we shared. Reese was so happy and grateful for our family, our relationship, and how close she and I had become in our adult years. She had begun telling me that she was sorry for what she had done while we were children. Love is all that matters, she stressed to me.

"Please make sure our loved ones learn this." She was so right. I had been feeling a little confused as to why she was suddenly so serious about this. So, I said yes to humor her at the moment. We went on with our visit, laughing and reminiscing about our younger years. It was truly a wonderful day. I went home with a smile in my heart, filled with so much love and joy. Later that same night, I was awakened from a phone call telling me to hurry to the hospital. Reese had died. Chills went up and down my spine. How could this be? I was just with her, and she was so happy!

I arrived at the hospital, and to no surprise, there she lay. Looking so peaceful. Reese is, and will forever be, with me in my heart. I am so grateful for all the love we shared that day. As we laughed, cried tears of joy, and prayed together at the hospital. She taught me to cherish every moment because it might be my last. This will forever stick with me. We all need to enjoy our loved ones while they are here with us; time is precious. Not one moment should be taken for granted, Celebrate the life you have been given.

I believe we need to be grateful for the lessons our loved ones share with us. Astonishingly, what she left me with was truly a blessing, not a loss. Reese will always have a special place in my heart. Our family was blessed to have her. I am so blessed because I have other sisters and an amazing relationship with each one of them now. Growing up, it was not always that way. LOL! (Laugh out loud) When they chose to act special, I had my extended family, sisters from another mother, and my besties. I now see that there is no loss. Reese lives in my heart, and she will always be with me. I am so blessed to have the precious memories of that day, and we have her beautiful, amazing daughters and grandchildren to carry on where she left off. God is so good to me.

ENEMY WITHIN

We are our own worst enemy.

It is horrendous to call ourselves names. Yet some of us start doing it almost every day, and then our day goes sideways, and we can't seem to get a handle on what is happening. I wondered why I would have copious days in a row, which were very challenging. I never referred to myself by name. I would ask myself, "Why did you do that?" Following it up with, "Are you stupid?" I then looked in the mirror and told myself that it was too hard to do it alone. I listened to other people who said it was hard and were afraid to put in the time and work to improve their lives and step out of their comfort zone, no matter how toxic. I know now that they were stuck in fear and that misery loves company, so they did not support me. As a result, I had myself convinced that I could not leave, and I was terrified to try.

I would come home every day to prepare dinner. I'd help my children with whatever they needed after we ate dinner. Then, I would sit on the couch, watch television, and eat junk food. It made me feel good, but after I was done, I felt horrible. Being anxious but not taking any steps to improve my circumstances, this went on for some time. Intriguingly, I noticed numerous people were also in the habit of belittling themselves. too. Constantly calling themselves feeble, despicable names. It was not until I began to get sick that I decided to take action. I had gotten big and had allowed myself to become larger than I was when I was pregnant.

Yes, it had become obvious to me that being our worst enemy had not only me but hundreds, maybe even millions of people, stuck. I had become bitter, and I did not recognize the woman I saw in the mirror. I was terrified to allow love in. I was so comfortable embracing the walls I had built up. I stayed angry at myself and life because, in my eyes, I was a failure. I was lost and drowning in self-hate, silently, for what seemed like decades. The enemy within was me. Repulsive as I may have been at that moment. I had to observe that I could make a choice and shift my direction. I had to stop hating myself and give love to me.

I had to decide to stop tearing myself down with my words. At the end of the day, I am for me, not against me. Nothing was changing for me. It was the same thing day in and day out. The battle within me needed to come to a head. I could no longer continue in pain. I was scared to make a move, but I began going back to the gym. Instead of dropping the kids off with a bag of chips in hand, telling them, I will pick you up later, I began to go with them. Working out gave me the courage I needed to tackle the enemy within. It was a start to loving myself and a healthier way of living, and it was the first step in evolving.

I was now going in the direction I needed to go in and beginning to live the life I wished to live.

I am not saying I work out every day, but I plan to improve each day. Taking each day as it came and making a good choice for that day, I sometimes got in a great workout, and other days, it just did not happen. I had to learn to take it one day at a time and not beat myself up when I didn't follow through. There were days it was a struggle, but I made up my mind that I was going to pick myself up and continue moving forward until I reached my goal of doing at least one mile of exercise each day. The enemy within still, at times, had a surplus of negative words I used to use daily. As each of those negative words was reconstructed into positive ones, I began to use only uplifting words. No longer am I my enemy. The enemy within is now for me, not against me. It did not happen overnight. It took lots of practice, one day at a time, one step at a time. I know if I can transform and improve, anybody can. I am now a friend to me; I have released the enemy.

FRUSTRATED

It is frustrating to wake up troubled,
with so many concerns on the mind.

I would wake up for years feeling very frustrated about so many issues, and each one made me very concerned. Although my life was in turmoil now, it did not mean I was blind to the world around me. I was frustrated about the lack of love given to some of the children in our world. Waking up troubled because a tremendous number of children in the world do not know unconditional love. I was seeing kids who are hurting and struggling because they don't have a village or community surrounding them, wondering: who is caring and willing to give them love? I was incredibly frustrated that it is unfortunate that not all parents are good parents. When their child falls, needing guidance, often there is no one there to give it.

They are frustrated that there are so many unhealthy families trying to raise healthy children with a lack of skills and tools, doing the best they can with what they know. They do not understand that the skills are missing. When there is a moment where healing can take place, they lack the love that is needed to change the trajectory of their family from fear to faith. Instead, they are doing something in the moment, ultimately causing more pain. However, healing steps could have begun if they had acted from a place of love and kindness. Sadly, the fear causes them to act out of rage. I was frustrated that when we are hurting, dumb stuff comes out of our mouths, and we sometimes act from anger, unfortunately causing more pain.

I know I have had my share of freaking out moments where I did and said things I later regretted. It was pure frustration and the regret of my bad behavior that helped me to see the error of my ways. Feeling shame for my actions helped me to realize I had to find a new way to handle my stress. There would be no more freaking out over every situation that comes. I began making a choice to stop handling the struggles life threw at me in mean, hateful, and unforgiving ways. Feeling very frustrated, I chose to make a vow to myself: I would work on myself and the bad habits that I had acquired while suffering from my depression, one at a time.

When I was about 26, I took in a child in need; loving her as my own explains why I am frustrated that there are children in the foster care system who are placed in unhealthy homes, hurting - mentally, physically, and emotionally. They are suffering from domestic violence, neglect, and abuse in silence; in search of someone to listen to or show concern, they long for someone to see them. I am powerfully praying that awareness is brought to these issues because domestic violence is damaging to our spirit, and the effects last a lifetime. It needs to stop. Frustrated but determined to become someone who brings awareness and helps to give love to the community. I began connecting volunteering in the community with organizations and people who can assist those suffering from life's traumas to services that will assist them in the healing they need, in a place where they can feel safe, begin healing, and where they won't be judged. I began my journey of volunteering in the community doing walks to raise awareness.

Frustrated that some foster homes are in it strictly for the check, it is a compassionless home, leaving the children to feel alone, unwanted, and depressed. I am certain that this system does not work and is in need of love. I was also very frustrated that some foster homes single out the children instead of including them. These children are people, too. They have feelings that should matter, and they need to be heard by members of the family, allowing them to feel included and a part of something special. I believe we need to stop referring to them as foster kids and call them by their names. By having conversations with others, I have had to learn the hard way that being referred to as a foster child makes the child feel like an outsider. They want parents to call them by name and refer to them as my child. This only makes sense to me. It is very frustrating to witness the amount of pain that so many children are subjected to. My heart ached not only for my children born to other families but for all the children in the struggle.

Frustrated yet determined to be the example of what should be done; although I was not perfect and I also made mistakes in my life and with my own children, I wanted to make a difference in other lives while going through my separation and later divorce. My niece, who was always with me, began telling me stories of the foster care system which she was currently in. It saddened my heart all this poor baby had endured in her short little life. She was broken and suffering. Frustrated, I thought to myself, something must be done. Someone must begin the healing. Well, we had a discussion, and she and I were done with our conversation, and it was clear to me that I was the one. My frustration caused me to make a move in another direction.

Allowing myself to leap from my comfort zone, I went from being a single divorced mother of two with a stepson, whom I adore as my own, to taking classes to be a foster mother. Adding one more thing to my already overloaded plate, I knew I wanted people to understand that kids are kids. Foster children can do well and be successful if they are truly loved, just like anyone else. I was a foster mother, and my children became my family the moment they began living in my home. I made sure they were aware that we are family. This is a bond for life. They were no longer a foster child; they had found their family. We are in this for the long hall - until death do we part. I find myself very frustrated that more people do not understand this concept.

Leaving so many foster children feeling scared that they may be abandoned at any moment and worried about what will happen or where they will go when they age out of foster care if they do not have a family who cares, I am frustrated that when they age out of foster care, many of these precious young adults have nowhere to go. I am determined to create a safe space for them to transition into as they learn how to move into adulthood. I am frustrated that there are many wonderful, fully capable men and women who want children yet can't conceive for one reason or another and that there are so many people blessed with beautiful, amazing, bright, creative children that they treat as if they are worthless. Why would God allow that? Or should I ask why we continue to allow this system to continue when it is broken?

There are those who could care less that they are blessed to be a father or mother figure, a teacher and mentor, responsible for shaping and molding someone special. Now understanding that everyone does not share my compassion or empathy, I am grateful to be blessed to live and grow with these amazing children God has put in my life. Frustrated that some stepparents do not give love to their stepchildren, I feel they fail to see that when they marry their partner, they take on the responsibility of their partner's children, too. It is not only about the relationship they are in with their partner. Frustrated, these types of people make the child or children feel like outsiders, instead of embracing and encouraging them, I am saddened they do not see the lifetime of emotional harm they cause the innocent children. I believe the adults' job is to help the children feel connected to the new family.

Disturbed that I have been in places and a witness to conversations stating, "You do for yours, and I will do for mine," my heart was breaking at the moment as I silently hoped for a compromise. I prayed God would help them to begin working together for the good of all the children in the family. I prayed for more tools to be available to teach families how to connect. As adults, it is necessary to create bonds with all members of the family in order to have a healthy family. Frustrated but determined to connect people to services that can bring about healing in a healthy way and where people can heal the way they need to and not be judged, I became an advocate for the community. I decided to be a voice of change and hope.

There are so many addicted children and adults who are barely coping with day-to-day struggles. Along with the shame and guilt of their childhood issues that were never addressed and desperately seeking an escape from the pain life has given them, they seek to make the pain go away in any way possible, many times through drugs or alcohol. People are dying; lives are lost because the fear of facing the pain is too much to handle; more needs to be done to address these issues. By helping to guide our children in the direction of hope and love, I believe we can help them get on the path to achieving the life that God planned for each one of us. Frustrated but determined to be a part of connecting youth to a place where they can heal and grow while they tap into their creative side, I lend my voice to them as their advocate.

I strongly believe with all my heart, if one child is hurting and causing harm to themselves or others, it should affect us all. We should make it our business to figure out a way to make a change. These children and addicted individuals are important to our evolving world. I believe we as a people need to be an example, exemplifying methods on how to handle stressful situations in a positive way. Someone can learn from each one of us. I truly believe becoming our best self is the gift we can give to others. We are indeed all teachers. We all have something someone else needs. I decided I was done waiting on the sideline for somebody to do something.

I choose to be a intentional in creating tools that help assist humanity in healing the harms in more constructive ways—each one of these concerns and frustrations. Children do not have a village or community or the feeling of unconditional love. Children being hurt physically, mentally, or emotionally. Men and women who can provide a beautiful home for children but can't conceive. Stepparents: making their children feel like outsiders, children, and adults dealing with addiction due to life pain, etc. It helped me realize there are so many needs in our world I could continue counting them up. It is a must that people work together. I became a foster mother for a reason.

I believe all children should know unconditional love. There should be a place every child can run to for comfort in times of trouble. Being a foster mother was truly one of the best things I have ever done in my life. I am now a mother of five beautiful adults and a grandmother to amazing children. I am so grateful to learn of Erie County Restorative Justice peace circle training practices. These practices are just what is needed to bring healing to our evolving world. They are bringing a healthy way to have healing conversations. Every time I attend, I always come out of them feeling refreshed and vulnerable. I am grateful to partake in facilitating on Thursdays at Eight Days of Hope whenever needed in the beginning and now due to our changing world virtually and in person at the ECRJC building in Buffalo on Hertel Street.

These training practices are great conversations that bring healing, and the methods can be taken and utilized in every area of life. Establishing my morning routine, along with meditation and prayer, helped me perfect the things that do not work and add new ones. I went from frustrated to faith.

I am embracing and learning to keep rising when I fall short. I plan to notice the issues of life that frustrate me and then create a plan of attack on how I can work on being a part of the healing. God has a plan for me and all my frustrations. I am so happy and grateful that through my community volunteering and training,

I was blessed to meet Kelly Whitfield and that later, we were led to have a powerful conversation about the mission God laid on her to create a safe space for people who suffered as she did from the traumas of life. This conversation later led us to partner up and I began to assist her in the community doing outreach. We bring healing lunches, hope, love, and more, connecting those who suffer from trauma to services and peer-based workshops at The Healing Hub Of New York. This is another positive way I could focus my negatives into doing something that brought others so much joy—turning my frustration into healing. I am now grateful to be a forever learner and giver by being a part of our healing world, bringing love to everything I do, and by giving food, love, hope, and healing to our communities in wondrous ways.

HEARTBROKEN
Being heartbroken leaves us empty
and feeling as if we are alone.

As I look back on my life and where I am now, it is clear that I was heartbroken and very depressed. Waking up heartbroken is awful. Pretending it does not hurt is worse. No matter where you go or what you do, the heartache follows. Nothing anyone says makes you feel any better. Therefore, you fight it by wearing a big fake smile, laughing, and doing what is necessary to get by, usually hiding by self-medicating with the drug of choice. mine was food. Sugar, in fact, and we had quite a relationship for many years.

My depression was like an up-and-down roller coaster as I moved rapidly through life's altering challenges, crying all the time over every little thing.

I desperately needed something to mend my broken heart. It seemed as if the food was the only thing that made me feel happy. The more I ate, the happier I became; food just tasted so good. It helped me to lose myself, forgetting for a moment how much pain I was actually in. The good feeling transmitters were igniting. Every time I filled myself with those sugary foods, I was happy, for the moment, anyway, but it did not last long. After the food was eaten, I went right back to being heartbroken.

Although I may fail when I try new things, usually by starting and stopping many times over, I promised to give myself some love. I am worth it. I vowed that I would not give up on myself; I would put a wall around my heart and move on. Protecting myself from more heartache, taking the steps, and then making the choice to give love to me first was a life-changing moment for me. Comprehending that life does get better when you decide you want it to.

We have all been heartbroken at one time or another. We may experience the loss of a loved one, a job, a relationship that went bad, or a dream being crushed. But I learned that it is not what happens that determines where you go; it is truly how you choose to react to what happens that makes the difference. I now choose to respond in love.

Our hearts break from challenge to challenge, but love heals our lives if we release the pain and bitterness. Louise Hayes helped me understand this. It is true that I become stronger as I allow what is instead of fighting it. I have grown and gone from heartbroken to happy with who I am becoming.

FREAK ACCIDENT

A life is lost but never forgotten in the
right place at the wrong time.

It is atrocious that you can be minding your own business, doing your daily routine, coming or going to a place you have gone to regularly, then abruptly, out of nowhere, a freak accident can take your life. This is exactly what happened to one of my very dear sister-friends. Feeling angry, explosive, frustrated, hurt, and so many other emotions all at once, I honestly could go on and on about how upset this horrible tragedy has made me feel.

This beautiful woman was a true queen, and she was always helping someone feel better about who they were. We would hang out with our children as we celebrated life's precious moments together. We had a strong connection because we had known each other for years through other family members. Our children are more like brothers than just friends; they grew up together and always encourage one another as brothers do. It was funny at times because there were three brothers and three brothers; the two oldest hung out, and the younger ones paired up too. We would often all be together at one of the sports events because the boys would be on the same sports teams. This worked out great because we would take turns preparing meals for all of us to eat on the go and making sure our children and others did not go without a meal. Often, at times, it was like our kids had two moms; as they say, it takes a village to raise children, and it is so true.

She made the best fried chicken, and the football teams loved it. In fact, even their families would be so excited, anticipating the moments when they knew it was her day to bring it. It was truly a relationship that would have lasted our lifetime. Everyone who knew her absolutely loved and adored her. When I think of what happened to this day, it still sends chills up my spine. It was devastating how this freak accident took place. This traumatic incident was a freak accident that should have never happened.

When we received the news of this freak accident, it was horrible because it was all over Facebook. None of us knew who it was at first, but everyone was talking about it. In the moment when it took place, I was on our porch with one of my sons. He looked at Facebook, told me what had just happened, and showed me the status. It was heartbreaking and brought us to tears. Instantly, I began to pray for the family and all connected to it. Never in my wildest dreams would I have ever thought that this freak incident would have had anything to do with anyone I knew and loved dearly. It was not until the next day that we discovered the woman's identity we had prayed for. It left us speechless and mortified. In just that moment, our hearts were broken, and our families' lives were disrupted.

There were no words that could explain or take away the pain we were now all experiencing and suddenly submerged in. I could not handle this, so I knew our children and families were feeling the same. This sucked, and it was definitely one of the worst moments in time. All I could do was let go and let God lead me so I could be there for our loved ones. Knowing this was not going to be easy to get through and only time would help us come to terms with what had happened. She left behind beautiful, amazing children, grandchildren, family, and friends. This is awful and so unfortunate, and now a fact of life we are forced to have to deal with. Freak accidents happen all the time; it just is not fair to be steeped in so much pain. At the time it took place, it felt like the pain would never stop. I just wanted time to stop for a moment and for everyone to go away. As I tried to understand why? Why did this happen? Of course, there was no explanation as to why this had to happen and turn our lives upside down.

This freak accident almost sucked the life out of us. We had to adjust and drag ourselves through. Until we found the engines that helped us move along, we all suffered and still have moments when it hurts like hell. Looking back at the precious memories I shared with her helps me keep moving forward and filling my heart with so much love. Freak accidents are just that; we have no control. I had to forgive the person who caused it and then meditate and pray—allowing God to work it out for me.

Understanding that we will never get over this, but we will, in time, learn how to go on with our lives, adapting to what took place and learning how to keep progressing even when freak accidents of loss take place that cause death, challenges, struggles, things taking place in life that I cannot control, etc. This life is not easy and a true battle to navigate, but it is still good and worth living. She taught me that. Just thinking of her smile and her laugh puts a smile on my face, and in my heart, her laugh was contagious. She could make anyone laugh in the worst of times, and she always did. She was an inspiration to our lives, and she always said no matter what goes on, it is a good day to smile and be grateful for all that our lord has blessed us with. She wore her faith on her sleeve, and she prayed every day.

Anyone who knew her loved her, and you were happy to be in her presence. She was the type of woman who would give you the clothes off her back if you needed them and would not think twice about doing it. She loved giving and serving others and always did something for the community. It was truly an honor to know her and love her. She is a true example of how to live a full life filled with joy in everything you do and is not afraid to take risks. Whenever you saw her, she was smiling and lifting someone else up when their spirit was down. She also helped me get through some tough times as we leaned on one another.

I am so grateful for every precious moment spent with her. Whenever someone passes, she would say this is not the time to be sad, but to smile because you know their memory lives on in your heart. Then she would do something crazy and have me laughing to the point I would almost pee my pants. She was amazing, and I will take her advice, smile, and trust that she is with us and will forever be in our hearts and memories. Freak accidents do happen, and this beautiful lady taught me how to move through with love.

DEPRESSION

It was hard working through my depression
and trying to hold it together.

As we dart off from place to place when we juggle our stresses of life horribly, we become feeble, and depression sometimes sets in. It is not acceptable in the world we live in to be out of control of our lives and our emotions. Depression happens and has become very much a fact of life for so many of us. At one time or another, I do believe each one of us has experienced some level of depression, is in depression, or is loving someone through this stage of life. No one wants to be in it or deal with it. I didn't realize I had checked out of my life and slipped into depression. All I knew was life felt like a brick house on my chest. The load felt unbearable, to the point I could not force myself to act.

Depression was something I heard about and did not quite understand. It was something that happened to other people. There was absolutely no way I was depressed, so I thought at that time.

I am unsure of when it started. There were numerous stressful situations taking place all around me. Copious amounts of my loved ones were managing depression and being medicated to help them cope. There has been so much violence and death surrounding us that it is almost impossible to escape seeing it.

It is no surprise so many are depressed, especially if you watch television. I have never felt so overwhelmed turning on the television as I do today. I believe this world of negativity is the cause of our fears. I believe television and social media are why people are scared, depressed, and not knowing what to do or who to believe. I am sure the stress I was under caused me mine.

Over the years, I have observed that not everyone has someone to talk to or seek advice from in times of trouble. Even when I felt stuck, my strong faith helped me begin to pray again. When I realized I was in a dark place and was on a downward spiral, it hurt so bad I cried. I asked myself, who is this person I see in the mirror? The person I am staring at is not me. I don't see me; she is depressed.

Now, as I look back to see what led up to my depression, I see it was a series of things: My broken heart, being a single mom, having to worry about starting to date again, and being terrified to open my heart again, along with going through the other traumas in my life and watching my loved ones experience it, too, was hard enough. Add to that the lack of money to do the things I needed for my family and just barely making it by living from paycheck to paycheck; I was fearing how to pay for the things we needed and robbing Paul to pay Peter all the time. These were just a few reasons off the top of my head that probably contributed to me being depressed. I still could not believe it was happening to me.

One day, after losing my sister, my other sister and I were looking at pictures when I asked why I was not in a picture I should have been in. My sister looked at me confused and pointed, saying, "That's you, right there." I was shocked, and I did not recognize myself. Later, as I sat in the dark, the shades were pulled down when it all raced through my head. I thought of everything that was happening, that had happened, how different I looked, and I felt that I was getting worse. I knew then that I had to do something. Falling into depression was a slow process that I could no longer ignore.

Finally understanding that I was depressed and stuck in my mess, I began desperately wishing I could help my loved ones through their own struggles with depression and anxiety. I knew I had to finally do something to make a change, and it had to start with me; I had to find my peace.

Understanding that depression is a serious issue that must be addressed, or it can become a slow death if not handled with care. I am no professional on depression, but I am not blind to the fact it has its grip on me and many others. I am sure the stress I was under caused me. It also caused me to check out of my life somewhere in the middle of the struggles. I was desperate and felt I must try something different. I began to pray as I was taught to do. I needed to call on that precious name of "Jesus," there is something special about that name that gives you a sense of peace.

Then, I spoke with my beautiful mother, who suggested I read Louise Hay's "You Can Heal Your Life." By doing a little breathing meditation daily and then adding this good reading, my mother said it would help get me moving. I began reading it first, then started listening to it as an audiobook so I could hear it in different ways. Finally, I realized affirmations do work - if you use them. I replaced all those nasty negative words I had with positive statements. Now, I am praying and repeating positive affirmations every morning. I imitated things I was reading and learning, such as pretending I was running on the beach as Tony Robbins was while screaming out his affirmations. I screamed out mine as I walked an hour to work every morning and then again on the hour going home every night.

I began to utilize the book along with meditation, prayer, and, most of all, gratitude, applying them as tools for a better life for me. I was praying I would be done with pain and depression soon. These tools would begin helping me to heal my life and become a better mother. My children are the most important thing in my life, and, at first, I had to do this for them and our loved ones until I realized the most important person to do this for was me.

To my surprise, I was interested in learning. Looking back, this is funny because my aunt is a forever learner whom I never understood. I took shortcuts to learning, but now, it is a kind of obsession, learning new things to improve who I am. I started going to Barnes & Noble and sitting quietly for hours, reading books for free. I began to feel better as Barnes & Noble became one of my favorite places to be. It was my secret oasis. While at Barnes & Noble, I became familiar with some of the greatest mentors.

Listening to Tony Robbins's Audio helped me to learn to create an hour of power and to become disciplined with the beginning of my day again. I noticed that all my mentors stressed the importance of how we begin. Jim Rohn taught me to begin disciplining myself, in one thing at a time, and master that thing before going on to something else, becoming an unshakable character by mastering the self in things first. Les Brown taught me it's possible to create the life you want, and you have to be hungry.

Oprah Winfrey taught me that you can start with nothing, go through unbelievable tragedies, and still live a good life if you believe you can. Her talk show was amazing and taught me many lessons. It was Oprah who also encouraged me to begin reading books that teach. Growing up, seeing a beautiful woman of color on TV who honestly cared about helping people was empowering.

Wayne Dyer taught me to chill out and allow by understanding we are more powerful than we realize. It is important to watch over our words and connect to our oneness, which is the God within, and to understand that we have all we need within us. Understanding and believing this helped me to stop searching for something outside of me. My mom always told us this, and now I finally believe it. This is the truth, and now, it is what I believe.

Jack Canfield and Lisa Nichols taught me to set goals and create abundance in all areas of my life while assisting me in learning to read books and then to set a one-year, five-year, and ten-year plan for achieving my goals. I started this over and over several times before I finally sat down and committed to writing it out. I also began creating a bucket list of dreams I would like to experience. I learned the importance of being your own motivator and building yourself up and that we all have something to give. These teachings helped me to realize that even if I am depressed or going through tough times, I have the strength and knowledge to start over every day, and I can overcome and still have a good life.

It was President Barack Obama who taught me to keep my composure even in the most stressful situations. From him, I learned to stay focused on the goal and that we do not have to lose our self-control to get our point across.

Billy Allsbrook taught me that I am blessed and unstoppable and motivated me to become my own champion.

T. Harv Ecker made me stop fearing my money, look at it, and begin to manage it. Though this did not happen overnight, and I still struggled with it, both T. Harv Ecker and Tony Robbins planted seeds and made me begin to face my fears with money. I noticed this issue always gave me high anxiety, so I would avoid it like the plague.

It was Bob Proctor who turned on the light, teaching me about paradigm shifts and the power of our paradigm. This was a great lesson. It hit me, and I started paying closer attention at that moment. I set my mind, and I was preparing to meet Bob and thank him for all his years of study and his passion for helping others learn this. Once I understood it, I knew he was right, and I began changing my life.

John Assaraf took me on the road to training my brain for success, allowing me to receive what I want and believe that I deserve it.

Mel Robbins and my beautiful granddaughter taught me to act before my brain causes me not to. Utilizing her "five four three two one rule," I began with a five-minute gratitude prayer meditation and then jumped up out of bed. I then began going downstairs in front of my television and began the one-mile walk with Leslie Sansone. This energized me to get through the day more positively. I am grateful for Leslie, the founder of this program; she is a truly amazing and inspirational beauty who has changed my life. I needed something easy and fun because, like I said, I was depressed. She taught me that ten to fifteen minutes is all you need to get a good, one-mile workout before you leave the house every morning. It gets the juices flowing and stimulates the heart, body, and mind, assisting you to be successful and at your best.

I am grateful for my aunt, who bought the DVDs for everyone in the family; these are what I use every morning. I have learned so many valuable lessons from my mentors. I now understand that everyone is a teacher, and that includes me. I am willing to continue being taught and learning throughout my life journey. I am grateful for my mentors and all their stories and lessons that have helped me and continue to help me. It is because of the tools from my mentors that I am free of depression. It was the tools learned and the courage to take the action steps in my own life. I am making life better for me and all my loved ones. I am on fire for life, and I have gone from fear to faith in just about all areas of my life.

Now, I am willing to tackle one struggle or challenge at a time. Facing what scares me the best way I can, when I have observed I failed, I use these tools to keep getting back up stronger, Believing in God to bring me through and lead me to my greatest good here. As I choose to give love to everything I encounter is my new way of living. Changing the habits I had that were not productive. I want more for myself and those that I love. Therefore, I will utilize the new tools and leave my negative thinking, bad habits, and depression behind. Praying that if I can learn to do it for myself, others can, too. Just maybe, following some of my steps, releasing and lifting that spirit of depression into hope and healing.

NOISE

When life becomes overwhelming,
we have to focus and tune out the noise.

Sometimes, life can seem meaningless when we have so much on our plate. It becomes vital to tune out the noise and focus on the goal we have set.

There always seems to be that individual who will not shut up, who is in your face constantly, trying to tell you how to live. That person always has something to say but does not say anything of value. They are not doing anything worthwhile for themselves but think they have all the answers. They continuously say mean and hurtful things to others, thinking it is funny, while the person they hurt is continually struggling, left feeling shame. They know you are on your game and are determined to move you from where you are. They keep calling you after you have already explained to them that you must make some changes, which do not include them now.

I found out. It is easy to get sucked back into old habits that make you retreat if you don't stick to the plan when trying to move ahead, being sick and tired of waking up where you are. I had to train myself to tune out the noise of toxic people and situations, to allow them to do and be what they are and not agree with or take part in what they are doing. I had to choose to stay the course, not let anything or anyone stop me from achieving my goal, and keep a positive attitude while on my journey.

I was a negative and very toxic person when I lost my sister and then my three-month-old nephew (that innocent little angel). Did he have to leave us? His loss caused our entire family so much pain, looking at life in total disbelief. It was clear everyone was trying, desperately, to find a way to manage their pain.

Then my son went to a house party that went crazy with gun shooting, and everyone who attended had to run in fear for their lives, trying to get out. Our family and friends rallied together in prayer at the hospital as we awaited the news. We were all grateful that all who were shot were saved by the grace of God. For a moment, it was one thing after another. These life-altering events had seemed to become a normal thing in the lives of so many. I could see how things could become very ugly if you allow your emotions to get the best of you and do not tune out the noise.

Many lives could be destroyed just from one bad choice made in the heat of the moment, especially when it is made in anger. I believe it usually only causes more trauma to an already very stressful situation. The stress these events caused our families has forever changed our lives. From these events, I became angry and frustrated in search of a tool or tools to help me.

I needed something that could be used to help stop my anger from escalating and allow me to tune out the noise of life so I could think clearly and focus. These devastating events had my wheels turning.

I knew if it was hard for me to digest, it had to be overwhelming for my children. It was imperative I had to tune out the noise and find tools that were positive and worked to help me get through life's unexpected events. I could then begin to teach my children and loved ones. Once again, as always, it was clear to me that meditation is something that works. When I quieted myself down and connected to my breath, becoming one with the God that lives in each of us, I instantly began to calm down and automatically tuned out the world's noise.

Life is not always fair, and if we do not learn how to tune out the noise, we will never know how to navigate through our life challenges in a positive way that does not hurt us or anyone else. Things are going to happen that we do not plan, but it is how we respond to life that matters. I do now believe learning how to stay focused and tune out the noise of life is essential to our well-being.

TEMPTATION
We all have a weakness.

I believe every one of us has a weakness. We juggle life trying to be on top of our game, sometimes taking on way more than we can handle. At times, we fail to recognize that each task desperately needs to be tackled but do not have the slightest idea how to work it out. We tend to see only the big picture, start feeling overwhelmed, then get scared and allow fear to creep in a while, thinking, "This is too much for me to handle." Moments like this made me paralyzed with fear, it was when I would search for instant gratification. This is how I lived after my divorce, and because I lacked discipline, the things that tempted me were what controlled me.

I gave in to what felt good, not thinking of the consequences because the pain in my heart took precedence over everything else. I would finish eating that cheesecake, ice cream, a bag of chips, etc., feeling guilty when I took that last bite. I would be furious with myself for not being conscious of what I was doing. I would then promise myself I would never do this again and last until the next obstacle crossed my path. This became a pattern I followed for almost a decade and a half. There will always be something that tempts us to do things we know are not good for us.

It wasn't until I learned to give love to myself first and then allow myself to feel safe that I tried to take on the task of life. Tony Robbins taught me to start with an "Hour of Power." He says to take the first hour of every day by creating a routine that works for you. The goal is to center yourself and start from a place of peace. It was not easy disciplining me to do this. I was not strong at first and had to keep starting over. It is how I overcame some of those weaknesses by allowing myself to release bad habits and the things that used to tempt me.

I acknowledged that I may fail at first, but it is okay. I reminded myself, "Just do not give up; keep trying until I figure out what works for me." When I tweak my morning routine to something that works, I get up and do it. I always knew prayer and meditation helped to calm me. Why was I not doing this on a regular basis? I do not know, especially since my mother taught it.

I decided to create my own "hour of power" and begin every day doing it. I am no longer trying to do everything myself, but instead, I learned to allow what is, (because I cannot control everything) by surrendering all to the God within me through meditation, prayer, and a good sweaty workout. I finally began trusting that it would work out just as God sees fit. Temptations still come from time to time, but I now can handle them a lot better.

CHANGE
We have to be the change we want to see.

Change was something I feared most. I was terrified of it. For many years, I kept everything the same. Mother gave us structure growing up, and this was a good thing, but it did not prepare me for our world rapidly evolving at the speed of light. I am grateful for my mother, who did her very best, sometimes taking the role of both mom and dad. She was strong and stern. Mom built us up and gave us the tools of prayer and meditation to navigate through life. Doing the best she could with what she was given, I did not realize these were gifts until much later.

My father also taught us lessons on how you can change who you are if you do not like what the choices you made brought you. He gave me the clarity to understand that we will not escape. We have to open the door and face the things we create from our deliberate actions. For every action we make, there is a reaction. I am so proud of my father for acknowledging the poor choices that caused him to lose the love of his life.

Grateful, he chose to change his ways, that we're not good, learned from them, and moved forward. Giving his life to God and being accountable for his former poor decisions, he made a conscious decision to change his life for the better after he was released from prison many years ago. He allowed himself to become the world's greatest granddad and dad to many. His transformation has saved many lives, and our family has a beautiful rainbow coalition.

My husband from my second marriage has blessed me, teaching me to adapt to change.

He did not have a stable childhood; things were always changing for him. This allowed him to learn not to get too comfortable with where he was in life because he knew it would be changing soon. He was just the medicine I needed, feeding me words of encouragement with his many very special pep talks: that is the word I am using. Lol (laugh out loud) but later gave comfort. Today, I am so grateful to have embraced all the changes that have taken place in my life. They have brought me to this moment. I now realize those difficult changes brought growth, maturity, and blessings. I now eagerly choose to be the dynamic I wish to see, empowering, improving, evolving, and forever learning.

TRUTH

What do you believe in?
What helps you in times of despair?

My truth is my strong faith. However, it was not always what I went to in times of despair. There were many years when I tried to fill that void with material things, the arms of a friend with benefits, a half-gallon of ice cream. This was my true weakness, or a nice size cheesecake. I even went so far as to hang out at the dance clubs with friends because I love to dance, and I had just enough drinks to make me feel good so I could drown out the pain. Going home to face where I currently was in life did not give me a feeling of joy.

These methods felt good in the beginning, but that feeling never lasted, and I did not wish to cause other problems by drinking too much. After all, drinking was what destroyed my marriage, the loss had my life turned upside down. I was searching for a solution to this new life. Therefore, I desperately needed help from someone who had answers, not someone who was not doing any better than me after going through trials and trying eagerly not to feel anything else. I decided to open my heart and try God.

I let God into every area of my life, finally utilizing the greatest tool I was given to call on by my mother. It wasn't until years after my great-grandmother's death that I truly began to understand that God is the beginning, the end, the Alpha, and Omega, as it says in the Bible. The teachings of Great Grandma began to set in. God is everywhere and gives me peace if I begin to live from that as my truth. There is nothing I can't do, but I must put in the action steps (prayer). I am now believing that God is guiding me every step of the way.

Trusting I am divinely guarded, protected, and covered by the precious blood of Jesus—we were taught this, and it kind of scared me as a child. I didn't understand that the blood of Jesus was a good thing and represented protection. Why would I want to be covered by the blood of Jesus? The teachings of Jesus later opened my eyes to this being a blessing, but it took me decades to believe I needed Divine protection living in this world.

It wasn't until I experienced possibly one of the worst moments in my life - my son being almost arrested as I was walking up to the scene, witnessing guns drawn and focused on my child. Terrified in the moment it all became a blur. Instantly, I remembered to call on the name of Jesus whenever you are afraid or unsure of what to do. So, I began to pray and believe God would protect us when the situation suddenly, calmly, unfolded peacefully right before my eyes. I realized I had been taught to pray and believe in God, but I was trying so hard to handle life and all the struggles myself. My children's teenage years it made me realize that it does take a village to raise children. I began to pray and call on the name of Jesus like never before. I now believe God is always with me, and I am truly grateful.

I have learned to call on Jesus, trusting and leaning on my faith to bring me through. Over the years, my faith has deepened and brought me peace, a feeling I could never have imagined. At first, I just did prayer from time to time because it was what we were taught. As the years went on and life kicked me around, I realized more and more I needed to pray all the time, not just when something bad happened. Beginning and ending every day with prayer is how I started, and then prayer became a conversation. Talking to my Heavenly Father throughout my day helped me to get through the tough times.

When I felt as if I just did not want to be bothered, I could always talk to God. I knew he would not hurt me and would always be there. I couldn't believe it took so long for me to realize this. I guess it is better late than never as they always say. I will forever be learning and continue to grow in faith. I am grateful to see that there are churches that teach the truth about how abundant our Heavenly Father is. I now stand in my truth; it is how I get through this world without being stuck in fear.

THE MIND
Our mind is powerful and precious.

Learning how powerful my mind is has given me a new outlook on life. I had never thought about it before. It wasn't until I began reading and listening to audiobooks that I understood and utilized the information. Like most people, I just went along. When I began perceiving the reason, I was stuck in a state of fear because of what I allowed to enter my mind, I just could not believe it was that simple. I had to try and see for myself. I eagerly decided to say yes to life. Recognizing that my choices would begin to make life better for my children and loved ones just by choosing what I allow and not accepting the garbage.

So, I decided to stop allowing myself to get up in fear. Stop feeding my mind the fear-based news and searching for the bad in the newspaper. Both are good tools if we use them properly. Mom taught us that we all have a special gift God planted inside us after reading and understanding how our mind works. For the first time in my life, I now believed this. Mom was right. Now, seeing for myself, one of those gifts is our beautiful mind and the power to use it however we choose.

With that being said, I promised myself to try to be positive again, start by telling myself nice things, begin to pursue me, and then try to figure out what my gifts are. Allowing only the best in I believed this would help me. It is our job to pay attention so our minds are not contaminated. Trust that if it is not teaching me something that will benefit me and others, I am not going to let it penetrate my mind. I will no longer accept subliminal messages that try to encourage what others want in my life. I am the keeper of my mind and excited for what is to come. Now that I am aware of how important this is. There will be no more programming of this mind. If it is not lined up with God, it is not welcome here, and I will not accept it, and I do not care who it is coming from. Keep it moving because I am not accepting of your negativity and fear-based garbage. Peace, love, and light, thank you.

HOPEFUL

Sometimes it is hard to be hopeful when
there is so much pain surrounding you.

I have lived through many seasons feeling helpless and wishing I could remain in darkness, while just wanting to pull the pillow over my head, close the blinds and take the phone off the hook. I was constantly hoping the pain and heartache of life would pass me by especially in those times when I dared to try to love again. Risking giving your heart to another hoping they feel the same, to find out after, that they don't, and probably never did was not easy to handle. Desperately just wanting to know how to do this dating stuff. So scared not knowing where to begin.

Before I understood the power of prayer, I would pray to God to help me and send me someone loyal, kind, and compassionate. I did not know how to be hopeful because deep down inside I felt like I was dying. I had doubt in myself, I didn't feel worthy that God would hear me. Starting to date again was tough. I didn't know how to trust. I would start a relationship with good intentions, then find out that my partner had other intentions. Honesty was nowhere to be found. Being lied to and stolen from by a man that says he cares deeply for me, afraid to confront him but knowing I couldn't live with myself if I didn't, I realized it could get ugly and the relationship would probably end. I was right, it ended, I felt horrible but knew he was not someone I wanted to be around my kids, I was learning to set boundaries.

No one wants to be put on the spot when they have done something wrong. Thinking to myself, "I have to confront the situation, I am not so desperate to have a man that I will ignore my values." I was depressed, not crazy, although at times I was not so sure. I talked to myself often and told myself that If things don't work out, it just was not meant to be. Back to the drawing board, I will go. Although I was not where I needed to be physically, spiritually, or emotionally in my life, I was not going to just put up with anything to be honest. I had a wall up around my heart, anyway, so being alone was ok with me. I had my children.

I tried to remain hopeful while making one mistake after another, fumbling my way through. The day-to-day routines had to go on anyway. Being a mother did not stop because my heart was broken. I still had a job to go to so that I could provide and make life happen for my family. Hopefulness was not an option for years; I was just trying to get by and doing what was important for my children. Unfortunately, I was not on that list. Just coasting from day to day, often wondering to myself, "Will life ever be normal again? Whatever normal is!"

Thank God for family and friends who helped me to start a new chapter. My girls who I grew up with, who I couldn't get away from if I tried, and boy did I try, they just don't give up and are very persistent. They were always being real with me and giving unconditional love, even when I was in a dark place and not wanting it. They never stopped giving me hope, because I knew they would always be there, no matter how long it took me to come out of my space of darkness.

Grateful for the many lessons that I learned from my great grandma regarding my faith - When all else fails, God will always be there she would say. Just call on the name of "Jesus" and watch how your situation changes. This is probably the greatest tool in life I have learned. So why did it take me so long to use it and to believe it and understand how truly powerful this is? Well, you probably guessed it. It was what the elders told us to do. Therefore, I just didn't believe it was true at the time. At this point I always went right back to feeling miserable.

Finally, I was sick and tired of being sick and tired. I had enough. I would try doing something different, it would work for a bit and things would be ok for a while. After a while I would just go back to the way things were, I got too comfortable. Instead of things getting better with this method of doing things they got worse, and I became overwhelmed. I decided to put my faith to the test, trusting that God has me; no matter what. He was preparing to dig me out of the hopeless hole I had allowed myself to fall in from my nasty attitude. I believe God used my children as a vessel to give me the hope to have the courage to go on.

I desperately wanted my children to learn the love of God - as Mom, Grandma, Moma (Great Grandma), and dad had so tried to teach us as kids growing up. I began to read Psalms every day while thinking to myself, Mom was right, we do usually go back to what we are taught. It is within us, and we can't help but do those things that are deep within. I was hopeful that I could begin again, despite my failed divorce and dating attempts. I had to just keep trusting in my faith, meditating on God's promises, surrounding myself with more positive people, and understanding that the church lives within us and it is important to lead by example.

Even when I felt bad, it did not mean I had to allow my negative energy in. I began to think of the things which bothered me and made me steer away from the church. What was it that upset me, causing me to get further and further away from what I was taught as a child? What was causing me to leave room for negativity and depression, causing me to feel hopeless for many years?

Suddenly, it came to me, it was some of the elders. They were nasty and very judgmental, while at the same time calling themselves holy Christians. In the same breath they talked about God and about what someone was wearing and how they look. They were judging, being very nasty and most of all angry towards those who did not fit their idea of how a "good Christian" should look and Instead of embracing them with love and wisdom, they made people feel unwelcome, so they did not return, which gave those elders the feeling that they, in their "superior" Christian ways, were right.

I never felt good about someone else feeling hurt and upset. It bothered me to see people in the church acting cruel. For the church to be the cause of pain, that just hurt my soul and turned me off to church. This incident stuck with me as a child. Being forced to be in church from sunup to sundown with Great-Grandma we would see a lot of different behaviors from the young and the old.

We were taught as children to be kind and embrace all people with love, while at the same time I was witnessing some adults with childlike behavior such as being nasty and cruel, in church. This just put a bad taste in my mouth. It made me want to detach myself from anything that causes pain to another, I now understand there are so many people in the church who are true warriors for God, but I believe it is those few causing pain that has the church pews empty today. I am hopeful that these individuals will learn to look in their mirror and give love to whatever they do in the name of God.

I had to begin to recognize that crap happens, no matter how good or bad we are. Struggles come even in the church, and we must deal with them. It is not what happens, but I have come to find, it is how we handle the situation that makes the difference. I had to stop being angry and mad at the elders in the church for being judgmental and nasty scaring me as a child. I also needed to stop being angry at my ex-husband and all those, who in my mind, hurt me. I was beginning to understand that they may or may not have felt like they were doing anything wrong. I had to accept that maybe they didn't know or realize what they were doing, so how could I judge them?

Learning from my trials and tribulations is truly what began to heal my life. It began by accepting things as they are and not the story I was telling myself. I cannot say how someone else is feeling or why they are doing the things they are doing. Maybe they were not trying to hurt me, but were just trying to survive, as I was. Understanding, I never intentionally wanted to hurt anyone, but I did, I just could not see it when I was in a dark place, it helped me to be hopeful and see things differently. I am now hopeful, choosing to live out my best life.

Praying I make the best decision for every situation and knowing that life is good because I choose it, I am very hopeful that I can reach and teach millions from my mistakes, my wins, and my losses. I feel that when we learn something that is healing to our life it is our responsibility to teach someone else, passing the good forward and inspiring others by giving them the courage to believe in themselves and then go after their greatness. In return they will start bringing hope to their family, friends, neighborhood, and community. I have learned in my life that hope is what heals lives and brings joy and the blessings God promised.

NEW DAY

After all of life's challenges, I have been given.
I am looking forward to a new day.

I am grateful for today and to breathe in the fresh air of a new day. Leaving all the feelings of fear and frustration, it was time to exhale. As I enthusiastically search for something new, I decided today is the day I choose to let go of the past. The past is the past for a reason. I know I cannot change it, but I can choose to create something good. Hoping to create my magnificent future, I have learned that I can learn from my past mistakes to forgive myself and everyone who has hurt me by releasing bitterness and anger, and by opening the door to a new day with positivity and gratitude. I am allowing this day, and every new day, to be a game-changer for me. There is no more holding on to the pain.

Releasing all negativity as I recognize it for what it truly is and humbling myself, calling on my Heavenly Father to help me control my big mouth, was a challenge for me. I have always been a person who likes to be in control; today, I am surrendering all. I am moving all negativity out of my way, allowing what is, letting go, and letting God lead me in the way that I should go. I am no longer in fear, but now, being present in faith, I am intensely claiming and commanding how my day should go. This is how I will begin the gift of every new day I am blessed with.

I am in charge of how my day goes and will start it with a smile. Although there are still many challenges that come my way taking me off course, I must remind myself that life happens, and it will kick you in the butt, causing all kinds of pain and painful situations. Life punches good people, too. I had to stop making excuses when struggles came and recognize how I behaved in the past. In the past, I would knowingly allow that unexpected challenge to be the reason to give up, and I would surrender to whatever direction the distraction took me.

I now choose to allow the distraction; it helps me to learn the lesson. Now, I understand that everything happens for a reason. Instead of reacting to the challenge, I have learned to utilize my tools, as I take three deep breaths and do a little meditation to help me get centered while keeping my original thoughts in mind as I move forward with love. Trusting and believing today is a good day, a new day, I now sincerely believe I am worthy to enjoy every new day as I see fit.

STARTING OVER
Getting started is usually a battle with self.

Getting out of bed was often the biggest chore of the day. As I forced myself to pretend I had everything handled, fumbling from one room to the other, I managed to get up and move. My morning routine consisted of me pushing it to the shower first. I did not want my children to see me crying since that was usually the first thing I did. I had to dry my eyes before they got up. I did not want them to see me and start their day worried about Mom.

I would then watch just enough of the news to catch the weather and tragedies. Sometimes, I would also find myself checking out the newspaper, looking to see who died. I would then leave, scared of what was happening in the world, as I headed out the door.

Trying to keep the normal routine when starting over after separation or divorce can be incredibly challenging. Working together was not an option in the beginning stages. It was like pulling teeth to have a rational conversation. Keeping all communication brief and right to the point was the best thing to do for quite some time. Although, I was scared to death of how I would do this on my own. I had to accept the fact that I was starting over. I did not have time to worry about it. As a result, there were many days when I had to wake my children up before 6 AM because I had to be at work by 6:30. Thank God my mother could help much of the time.

I had to make life happen for my children and me. I was grateful for my family, friends, and loved ones, but everyone had their life obstacles at the end of the day. I had to woman up. I became numb and went full speed ahead directly into mommy mode. Starting over was a battle I fought every day. I feared the words my husband said, "You will never make it; just come back, and I will take care of us," along with a lot of other profanities. I thought about it several times because it was hard. Sometimes, I had my back against the wall, trying to figure out what to do.

There was my pride - I had to let that go. There is nothing a mother will not do to meet the needs of her children, such as taking jobs you don't like to put food on the table and pay the rent, working sixteen-hour shifts four days in a row, looking forward to day number five when I had the three days off. I would put the kids on the school bus, race to the shower, and hit the sheets to get some rest while they were in school. Liking the job was not always an option, making the rent and keeping a roof over our heads was my focus and my main priority.

TAKING OWNERSHIP
Being responsible for what we do is important.

After my divorce, I was steeped in anger at my ex-husband. I blamed him for almost everything. I was devastated that my marriage had come to an end. I was full of hurt, and I had a tough time focusing. It was not until I began to shift my awareness from him to me. I could see I was at fault as well. I was agreeable at first, and that was the beginning. We made those decisions that changed our life as it once was. Leaving out prayer and going to church as a family, I had to re-evaluate my own choices, owning my part in what took place in our relationship.

Making the decision not to go to church and praying together, taking God out of the equation, was not a good decision. I did not understand then that we are the church and can pray wherever we are. Prayer is important for the success of the family. God should always remain the center. When I could bring myself to be accountable, things changed. For a smidgen, I could relate to my ex. The hair on my arms stood up. I never thought I would be admitting to such a thing as that.

Knowing the road ahead would be difficult as a single parent. I knew deep down that after things settled, my ex would eventually stop being angry at me for leaving. I hoped he would become who he needed to be as a dad to our children, learn to love himself, and cope without band-aiding with drugs and alcohol. As I prayed for him, hoping he would be blessed with someone to love and allow himself to be open for love again, I realized my parents divorced and are a fitting example that you can survive after divorce. It is possible you can have a good life, but it takes a lot of prayers. As I have said, I was heartbroken and very hurt and, at first, did not utilize my faith as I do now.

Realizing that children do not stay little forever, I decided that I would not live in fear; my sons would see this behavior as their normal. I did not want them to learn to party until you drop and think doing tht was okay. It is what many of us do in our twenties - we deal with life immaturely, but this was not something I could live with as normal behavior as a parent. It is unhealthy, and with no judgments on how you choose to live your life, I will not be joining you. At that time in life, I knew it was not about to change. No matter how hard I prayed and how much I begged my ex, it was going on deaf ears. It was becoming a pattern that did not sit well with my soul.

I never for once thought this would be my life. My heart felt betrayed, and my trust was gone, too. I knew when I fell head over heels in love with my ex-husband, that he had these issues with partying. I did not want to believe it was that serious of an issue. Everyone partied; it was the thing to do, but now that we had a family, we had to focus on re-evaluating our priorities. To be honest, he told me that he would slow down when we got married and that he would not do it anymore.

Call me crazy, but I believed him. I believed every word he said. I was taught that a man's word is to be honored and you know a man by their word. He was a good man, so I knew he would keep his promise. Well, I learned promises and hearts get broken when alcohol and drugs are added. My heart was broken, and I had to find the courage within. Realizing you cannot force a person to do what they have already made up their mind about. It was a hard pill to swallow, but I managed to swallow it. I am embracing what it takes courage. Because we have beautiful children together, I will never regret our life and have learned ignoring the red flags is not good, but I have vowed to never allow anyone, no matter how much love there is between us, to cross the boundaries and hurt me or my family.

I did not see it in me, but you must deal with what life throws at you when you are a mother with little children. You must pray and trust God to give you the courage. Only then can you begin to see who you have become and what you are capable of doing. I am grateful for the lessons I learned, from the pain I endured. I am grateful to experience the greatest love of my life, and for all that it has taught me, praying and trusting that God will one day bless me to know that unconditional heartfelt, passionate, blissful love again in this lifetime.

I decided, after going to counseling and trying to work with my ex-husband and his refusal to keep his word, to just see things for what they were and allow what is. I was done fighting this losing battle on my own. Learning that you cannot fight someone who has already made up their mind on what they are going to do is a hard pill to swallow, but life happens, and we deal with what comes at us. I am profoundly grateful for all the lessons I learned from our loving relationship. I am grateful to know a love like no other and to have experienced such passion and commitment.

I am forever blessed and grateful for every moment shared and each lesson from it. I took ownership of my life and the choices I made and decided I would not live in fear because of alcohol or anything else. When your partner continues to disrupt the home and the peace of everyone in it, it is time to embrace the situation for what it is. It was a hard decision, but my love for my own sanity, mine, and my children's mental health was on the line. This was my first love, and I had no idea what to do, but I knew this would not end pretty well if I did nothing.

I had to take ownership of how I would live my life and set boundaries on what I would or would not allow. I decided I wanted peace in my home. I was not going to be up all night because you decided that you were going to go out, get drunk, and come home, disrupting our sleep and behaving badly. I would just deal with it because you are my husband. I would be up all night worried about what might happen, afraid to go to sleep. Taking ownership gave me away out of the chaos and peace of mind.

EMBRACING AND ALLOWING

Embracing the oppression of our world
and allowing myself to be a part of the healing.

The first step in our healing is being mature enough to see our world's many challenges and oppressions, to feel the pain through those we love, and when it is me, take deep breaths. Be compassionate, empathize, and recognize that we do not always have the same beliefs; we must allow others to believe as they wish without judgment. Understanding that we all come from various backgrounds and what you embrace as your truth, I may not. Realizing I may have a chip on my shoulder because of the burdens I carry, I may come off a bit rough on the outside. I still deserve to be embraced with dignity and respect. I am doing my best with what I know.

The misunderstanding with the police officer who had mistreated me and my son in 2006 was a hard pill to digest. Being racially discriminated against takes a lot out of you. To add insult to injury, I had to pull it together, get up, and go at it as if nothing had happened. It took me years to embrace my emotions and process what happened. I had to remind myself there are still too many racist people out there who have learned to hate what does not look like them or where they came from. That officer had a hatred for people of color. I could not imagine what would make a person be filled with so much hate! It is taught at home that we are not born to hate. I passionately believe this and think it is important to learn more about others. I pray that people will begin to open their eyes and see that this is still taking place in our world.

Help people come together. We must see that what is on the outside does not matter. We are one spirit, one family, God's family, no matter what color our skin is. Come together and do what is right for the good of all.

The time for giving love, not hate is now. I believe we should use our voice to have conversations that bring healing at the grocery store, doctor's office, dinner tables, etc. These conversations are uncomfortable and needed to help open the minds of mankind. I believe every person, no matter the color of their skin, should be treated with dignity and respect. It should be an easy decision, a no-brainer. I could not believe in the year 2006, so many years after Martin Luther King Jr. had passed, that I was facing the same prejudice and hate.

How could things like this still be taking place? I always admired him for all he and the people of the time had to endure and how he embraced it with love, standing for peace for all. It was and is unbelievable to me that we are still dealing with these issues. With nothing being done or paying any attention to it, hate and racism is something that has been pushed under the rug for centuries and is still happening to black people and people of color.

I was angry, but after listening to Mom, I decided I wanted a peaceful resolution to this. She was right; it started with me. I had to forgive. Allowing myself to forgive helped me embrace the fact that he was raised to hate, and I was raised to give love. We were brought up with vastly different beliefs. Although he was in the police force, he had not learned that all people deserve to be treated with dignity and respect.

I did not want any more pain coming from this awful situation. I desperately wish it never happened and learned that this and worse happens every day somewhere. Realizing this made me want to throw up. Knowing, as a result, there are a lot of unchecked traumas in our neighborhoods and families. I could not change what took place in my situation or the past, but I could pray. God would create a way to bring about healing. As I began to embrace my emotions, I learned how to get through with peace and love. Praying officers and communities would learn to come together.

Even when we do not look like one another or share the same beliefs, people can learn to close their eyes for a moment to see themselves in someone else's shoes before deciding to be unkind or to judge. I had to allow an open mind to begin networking with many different people with amazing beliefs that do not always match mine. Volunteering and taking free training workshops in the community with community organizations that share a common goal, to create a world where we can all live together in peace has helped me in my healing journey. As we are all growing into greater, healing our world one step at a time was the beginning of a positive way to use my energy, giving love to my community.

I threw myself into giving love to everyone and everything in the evenings and some Saturdays, filling my time with these community organization workshops, which sometimes took all day. something was still missing. I had to allow myself to give love to me. I was embracing the fact that although this happened to me, I was worthy. I deserve dignity and respect, too. Meditation and prayer were the tools used as part of my healing morning routine. I also went to the Delaware YMCA to get a good workout on the weekends and weekday evenings. I gave myself a gift of two hours a day. At first, it was one hour in the morning and one at night. It began to help me in almost everything. I began to feel better and then felt I could add to my responsibilities and no longer crumble under the weight of pain. I was healing myself and my community.

Exercising was a great stress release and a fun family activity for the kids and me to do together. I was grateful to see them smile. It had taken some time for us to rise, as we were all depressed about this incident. Exercising helped us all have something good to focus on.

When it comes to healing, we cannot do it alone. I have learned we must come together as a collective body. It is not the red side versus the blue side, not the rich versus the poor, not the believers against nonbelievers, not the black, yellow, brown, or white; it takes each one of us to come together to do the work that is needed. Divided, we fall; together, we rise, but only if we can find it in our hearts to forgive and embrace our brothers and sisters with love.

I do believe we are one family - God's family - and we all belong to the universe. Every generation needs something to do to restore the harm caused by angry, hurt people, who may be our ancestors or loved ones. I am tired of seeing the results of what anger and retaliation bring.

Reacting to situations with hate only brings more pain and more painful situations for everyone to have to go through. It starts with me, and I choose life for my loved ones. Embracing love and forgiveness, not for him but for all those whom I love. Allow them to learn a new way to handle challenging life situations. I do believe that when you know better, you do better. I am choosing to forgive and utilize restorative justice practices to bring healing into my life. I am so grateful for these tools. I wish I had known of them earlier in my life, back when this unfortunate situation took place; perhaps we could have created a space for healing and a healthy conversation. Maybe I would not have had to go so many years holding on to the trauma. I am no longer acting from pain and fear but embracing and allowing, trusting God to guide me along the way.

WHERE YOU ARE AT
Acknowledge where you are and move forward with love.

It was very difficult for me to stop and face where I was in life. Acknowledging that would mean I had to be open and ready to deal with the pain life had caused me. My heart was not ready for that. I firmly allowed myself to feel nothing. In fact, for years, every day was just like the one before it. I silently went through the motions of doing my motherly duties. When I allowed myself to date, we did just what was needed to keep the relationship alive.

My walls were up, and my heart was heavily guarded. I was blessed that someone even was interested in trying to talk to me because I cried through everything. For a very long time, I had no desire to do anything. I thought being a good mother was all I had the energy for. Noticing where I had drifted was not easy; I was lost and felt like a failure. I had let myself go in just about all areas of my life. When I looked in the mirror, I gazed into an empty shell. The woman I once knew was not there.

Recognizing where I was and what I had allowed myself to become, that the traumas of life were hard, and that life had slapped me, I knew I could reach out, but I didn't know how or where to start. I didn't want to face life. I used to daydream of my future and how wonderful things would be. Well, things were not wonderful for me, and I could not see how life was going to ever be good again. After looking at my children growing like weeds right before my eyes, I decided I had to just start and begin where I am, trusting in my faith.

I thought to myself if I could somehow pull myself out of this place I was currently in life, maybe I could help someone else. I intentionally began to make the best choice I could for whatever I needed to do. I began living from my heart; if something did not rest well with my soul, I wouldn't do it. I started choosing to give love or give nothing while refusing to allow in any negative garbage. I have had enough of that. I made up my mind that I would be the love I needed for myself, my children, and all I met.

Trusting that the power that is in each one of us is what I would tap into, acknowledging and accepting that God is love, I began starting each day from a place of peace. I began quieting my mind by meditation and prayer, as my mother had taught us. I was finally allowing myself to line up with the God power within that connects us all, humbling myself so that I could live my best life. I began leaving judgments and negativity out and began believing that there is always a way to do things with love if we choose it. No matter how bad or good you think it is, where you are right now is the perfect place to begin. Remember that no matter how rough your life is, someone else may be going through something similar or worse and needs to hear what you say. Self-care and self-love are important to our well-being, and being grounded helps things to go much better.

My gift of love to humanity is writing this book as a healing for thousands of lives, hopefully even millions. It is for people who desperately need to learn how to give self-love and self-care. Your way of healing may differ from mine, but it is still important and will be the answer to someone's prayer. I am now peaceful in my life, even during difficult times. I have learned to embrace and allow what is happening now, there is no more fighting or pretending it is not happening. I recognize the situation; it may not look pretty, but by believing I can get through it and accepting that life is not always fair, it is still good.

WAKING
Out of Darkness into the light.

As I look back at my life, I realize that, at times, embracing life has been very challenging. Growing up, I was always a happy kid and, naturally, a very upbeat, positive person. I was always ready to take on life and all that it had to give. Just waking up was all I needed to be happy. Sometimes, I would notice other people looking at me strangely. They sometimes asked, "What drug are you taking? "In a kind of nasty but jokingly type of way. It did not matter what other people thought of me when I was in a good place. Honestly, I know I get it from my beautiful mother, who has always been a person of great wisdom, spreading love and positivity and living life with joy.

She would make us sing the song "I've Got the Joy, Joy, Joy, Joy, Joy, Joy, Joy, Joy" if we were feeling down, and it would always make us laugh. Therefore, I just could not believe that I was depressed. Waking up to that realization was very difficult. It had been almost two decades. I woke to the epiphany that I had been standing still, and everything was the same. For about seven years, nothing changed except my address, which was changed a few times. I made it look good on the outside, but inside, I was numb to the outside world. Waking up was not the problem; how I felt when I awakened was the issue. I was carrying the weight of life on my shoulders. There were days when I wanted to just roll back over and not even get out of bed.

It was so overwhelming, thinking about all the responsibilities, that were all mine and mine alone to deal with. The fear of life situations was running rampant throughout my mind, and I did not know how to stop the noise of life. It was simply too much to handle. I was escaping in food. Food had become my addiction. My cabinets were filled with goodies. I had replaced crying myself to sleep with cookies, cakes, doughnuts, and extra helpings of lots of good food. I stopped buying pants and began wearing stretchy and jogging pants. All that mattered to me was my kids. They were happy, and that was simply good enough for me.

This went on for quite a while until I began to feel weird. I was so stressed out between my divorce, dating, responsibilities, and life happening that I had no choice but to go on blood pressure medication. Then, I awakened to the reality that I was out of control. I never wanted to be the one to have to rely on medication, I'm not saying it is a bad thing; if you need it for some time to keep you healthy and balanced, then by all means, do it. Then take your life into your own hands and do what you need to educate yourself. As I was now forced to do because it got old, I woke up scared and stuck in fear. Not wanting to get out of bed, I desperately wanted to begin my day in a new way. I had begun watching and listening to audiobooks on YouTube.

I came across a five-minute meditation. Thinking to myself, "Oh! Mom would be happy if I did this. Just maybe this could be what is needed to jump-start me on my way to loving myself first, so I can start becoming the healthy person I need to be in order to function in this life." I then would close my eyes and begin to connect to my breath. Breathing into the count of four and out to the count of two, I was quieting my mind as Mom taught me to get rid of stress, negativity, and struggles. After reading and listening to some of my mentors. I realized Mom was right and on point. I guess sometimes we must get confirmation that what our loved one is telling us is true. I should have known; Mom knew her stuff. After all, she was always studying and reading something.

I decided to begin a daily routine of taking deep breaths, relaxing into meditation, and letting go of all the negativity of my day. Saying thank you and trying to feel good was the beginning of a new way of living. I was returning to my roots, utilizing the tools that helped me to feel better. It was a process at first and did not feel natural. I decided to keep on this path because it was working.

It is true that when you find one good thing and use it, another one follows. I was so tired of starting my day feeling lonely, scared, tired, and afraid. I now made up my mind that I would start my day in joy, even if I had to die trying. I was going to stop feeding myself garbage that made me feel horrible and be more careful what I allowed myself to take in. Smiling and finding positive ways to cope with my day-to-day rituals, now understanding that we must pay attention or take the risk of dealing with the crazy that comes, I learned to walk away and replace the hour in front of the television with reading a self-help book. I got back to journaling and listening to music.

Learned Optimism- How to Change Your Mind and Your Life, by Martin E.P. Seligman, Ph.D., was the first book I read in years. I had been allowing myself to dwell in darkness. Most of the time I was very lethargic and depressed! I only had the energy to turn on the television set and eat. After reading Learned Optimism, I clearly understood how things are learned and that I could change my behavior. The light switch was turned on. I realized that it was my pain and heartache that was causing me to self-protect because I forgot how to cope and reacted in anger and negativity. Waking to the reality that this was not who I am, but it was who I had morphed into, was exciting. I realized this does not have to be my life anymore.

I had been operating from a dark place and desperately trying to find my way out. It made me want to learn more. I could now see that being in the pain prison that I created for myself was not healthy. The funny thing is I never even realized I was behaving this way. It was like I woke up from a dream. This one book, the first of many, got me choosing to start my day with joy and a smile in my heart. It led me to do other things that also helped me. I continue to grow, and I keep getting better. I even started going to the gym again. Now, I did not say I was attending every day, but I was going. It took years before I became a regular, and now the Delaware YMCA is like my second home. I love and adore our Y –family.

I am grateful to have woken up from the darkness I lived in for decades and am eager to live and learn new ways to fill up and handle the stress and struggles of our world. I am now looking forward to and expecting good days and amazing new endeavors that are on the way.

TRUST IN GOD
I have learned that no matter what I have done,
God still loves me.

Learning to trust in God taught me that where I am today is not where I will end. No matter what I did yesterday or will go out and do today or tomorrow, I am not my mother or father; we are perfectly and wonderfully made for the purpose God planted in us, and I am loved. Each one of us has a purpose that no one else can do. Tony Robbins, Bob Proctor, Oparah, and all the great personal development coaches and motivators are right; we are all very important pieces to the puzzle. Our gifts are not for us. They are for our world to keep it evolving in great ways.

Our main job is to stop being so down on ourselves and forgive. Giving love to me first helped me allow my gifts to come forward. I can now be a part of blessing our world. Trusting in God gave me the strength to see that love is how we get things done. My first step was repenting and asking God to forgive me for being so bad to me. After forgiving myself, I could truly forgive others and start sending love instead of negative, angry, and unforgiving thoughts. I was my worst enemy for years. I then began letting go and letting God lead me.

I started each day with prayer and a five-minute meditation connecting to the God within. Trusting in God gave me peace, and life began to move in an upward direction. The movement of positive change began, and my life began to connect. I saw hope for the first time in years, allowing God to lead me in the way I should go. I am no longer fighting but lining up with the flow of life while making many mistakes along my journey, choosing to learn the lesson as I fall. Each time, I am getting back up stronger as I trust in God, moving forward, and grateful to keep on learning throughout this journey called life.

DON'T QUIT

It does get hard, but do not quit
because blessings are on the way.

My great-grandmother always said, "When you fall in love with Jesus and move your ass out the way, blessings are on the way to you." Therefore, don't quit. You will miss your blessing if you do and will have to start over. I managed to always keep this in mind. There were times when I questioned myself about these blessings. Why does it seem like right before any good comes, we are almost made to feel like we are dying as we experience a life struggle or situation that makes us want to quit because the pain is unbearable?

I can honestly say that is how I felt, and when I was depressed, I almost threw in the towel many times. Acknowledging that if I quit, I will never feel good about myself. This was my takeaway after watching some people who quit at life. Then they would make one 'bad' decision after another making it hard to follow through on other things that need attending. I know this because I was that person for a short period and watched friends and loved ones who also did this. I could only see the negativity when I was angry at the world hurting. It felt like the odds were against me all the time.

It wasn't until I made my mind up that I was not going to quit. It was not about me. I was thinking to myself - I have children, and if I quit this life, they would probably do the same. Although I was hurting and maneuvering my way through some tough times, I was not going to have that for my loved ones. I had to keep pushing and choose to keep going at life from different angles. If one thing didn't work, try something else. I always remembered why I was working so hard: to change the direction of my life. Doing that gave me the energy to keep moving when I wanted to quit. It was my belief in my faith, trusting God will bring me through, and holding on to the attitude that all things are possible with God.

Being a single mother in life was not easy. Quitting was not an option for me. I learned that it does truly take a village, a community, to raise children. I had to push myself even when I didn't feel like it. My children were my motivators and the real reason why I had to achieve success with the task at hand. God blessed me to be one of their dominant teachers because it starts at home. I decided even when I fail, I will get back up and keep on rising to the occasion every time. I continued encouraging myself and my children, letting them know things do not always work out how we plan. Don't focus on that - It is not what is important - keep getting back up until you win and do it with love; do not quit.

COMING TO THE LIGHT
Learning how to think is a gift from God.

I now realize when we are hurt, depressed, or going through challenging times in life, we often think differently, if we think at all. Sometimes, we go on wishing to be left alone as we drift off into the darkness, too afraid to face what is before us. For several years, I went through life just coasting and had no idea why. I could not see I was in a dark place at the time. It never crossed my mind that if I wanted to, I could do things in another way. I am not sure when it happened. Maybe it was the divorce, the shock of the experience with the police officer who racially discriminated against me, the death of my sister and nephews back-to-back, teen years with my children, etc., as I navigated my way through, every day was scary, not knowing which direction to go in. I desperately wanted out of this nightmare I lived, terrified, pretending I was ok.

It showed sometimes when driving, it was so hard to stay calm, I was always nervous. I was so afraid the officer was coming after me. Every time I saw a town police car behind me, I automatically froze up and could barely move. It was hard to sleep and to function. It seemed like the same day for years; nothing changed, and it wasn't getting any better. I could not seem to shake the fear. Even after we moved, it was still very hard to focus. It was tough being angry and hurt, feeling so alone. Yet, I was the one who had to hold it all together. My mom's encouraging me to meditate to aid me in quieting my mind and connecting with my breath finally took hold. In that silence, it came to me that I should read books. Reading books started me listening to audiobooks from some of the greatest motivators. I began to take a little from each one and began incorporating their methods into my daily routine.

I realize God has given us many gifts, thinking is only one of them and now my life keeps getting better. Life has become lighter as I come to the light, and I make better choices. It took some time for me to see if it was possible to move in a new direction. Although I still have many issues and a lot to learn, I now comprehend that life has many twists and turns. I am forever grateful. I can now see and believe there is a light at the end of every tunnel.

I am looking forward to and embracing each lesson I come to. Now, perceiving each path that I take brings more light to the darkness I once dwelled in, resulting in each day being brighter than the one before it. God has blessed me to be the light in my life so that I can light the path for someone else to follow.

ACCEPTANCE
I have learned to accept and allow what is,
no longer fighting my way through life.

After years of standing still in life, unsure of which direction to go in, I decided it was time to allow what is instead of being angry and fighting the life challenges that came my way. It was not an easy thing to do at first. It took me almost seven years to do this. Accepting the obstacles that came in life was difficult. Some people around me always seemed to have something to say about how I should address things. Sometimes, being angry at me because I was not aggressive enough for them.

At times, that made me feel upset because I never wanted to hurt anyone or their feelings. I decided to accept the things that have happened because it is what it is. I had to learn not to care about what people think of me. Allow me to do the things I felt in my heart that were good for me. At the same time, the haters will always have something to say because they are not courageous enough to do what makes them happy so they can become who God made them to be.

I was allowing myself to understand instead of doing what they needed to do. They get angry at you, having no problem pointing out your many faults and mistakes. They were afraid to look in their mirror. I convinced myself that I have tough skin and that I can handle it, choosing to ignore their toxic opinions about me and others. I was slowly distancing to hear my thoughts on what I needed to do for my life—accepting that if I did not wish to continue on this path, I needed to stop being afraid and face it. No matter how bad it was, I had to just go at it full force.

It can be tough when you realize that everyone you think is with you is not in your corner. Having to accept that you may be on your own. It hurts and can be lonely. When I started in another direction, no one else wanted to do the things I was doing at first. It was T.D. Jakes, who helped me with his motivational -Beware of 3 Types of Friends. It was an eye-opener for me. I believe everyone should listen to it, as I did, so you can truly understand who you are dealing with. Learning who is really for you and who is not.

After you listen to it and digest what is being said, you will never look at life the same. You will have a good understanding of people. This will help you to know what to look out for as we move on in our journey to understand who we are. It is only at that point you can accept with a clear mind that you are on the right path and that you are the one who is going to bless many, many people, most importantly yourself. When we stop trying to be someone we are not, we realize we all fail and make huge mistakes. I was so happy to learn this.

My mentors helped me to see we are all here to help someone else. As we help ourselves on our healing journey. Stepping into your greatness as you accept that you have the power to change whatever you need to. To have a life that works for you. I was so happy to learn new ways of handling life situations. The more we know, the better we do, and then we can pass our knowledge forward to help someone else along the way. Accepting me for who I am was the first step.

I am giving the best to me first. In the past, I never saw myself when I was in that dark space of pain and heartache. So I guess that's why, at times, my partner didn't either. Opening up to the truth, we all fear the person we see in the mirror at times. Believing others won't think we are good enough. We have to learn to accept ourselves as we are in that moment. I did and started from there, and then I began accepting others for who they are, not who they tell me they are. Learning to be aware and present in all my relationships has helped me to become a better person. We are accepting that I am worthy of having good in my life.

DREAMS
We all have something that makes us feel alive.

Our dreams are what make life worth living. They give us something to strive for, trusting that dreams come true if we believe in them. I have learned that if you are dreaming of something and thinking hard about it, that dream is something you need to make yourself sit down and pursue. I believe our dreams are important; they are gifts to the world.

Dreaming and praying that, though I failed at my first marriage, there is a great love out there for me. He was someone honest and true, dedicated, loyal, and committed to me and me only. I began praying for a man who was ready to love and be loved unconditionally. Little did I know, he was always right in front of me, walking with me, talking with me, and helping me through my struggles; he was my best friend. We dated off and on for twenty years before I trusted and believed in him, in us, enough to accept him as more than my best friend. I somewhat jokingly told him that if he was still around in twenty years, then maybe I'd talk about marriage. We have been married five years now.

Don't get me wrong, it has not always been easy, we have seen each other fall and get back up too many times to count. The problems were individual and with each other, but, amazingly, he was the one man who was always there, no matter what. He watched me grow, encouraged me, and listened to and with me, and our families have become one. In watching my growth and being my cheerleader, he has also found that he needs to grow to keep up with me. We may not be growing at the same pace, but there is hope as long as there is growth. I am so happy and grateful for all the life lessons we have encountered and that God loved me so much; he gave me a best guy friend who would stand with me through the storms.

Dreaming and creating a life we can be proud of also helps us dream of ways to serve humanity and helps us solve some of the problems. My dream is to fulfill one of those needs by exhibiting a detailed approach to how I learned to love myself again. Looking back and realizing that I was afraid to think of my dreams because they were out of my reach. I felt that I could not do them on my own and that only God could bring these dreams into reality. I always wanted to help millions of hurting people find a way to love themselves as they go from trauma to healing like I did. I hope I can bring them love and hope by allowing them to feel safe, and they can then feel good about themselves.

As a result, one of my strongest dreams is to feed one million people a healthy meal with a positive message to bring hope into their lives and remind them that they are not alone; they matter. I began going to various organizations to get trained in community outreach. I then began working with Miss Triggs, preparing and serving holiday meals and giveaways to people in need. Through Miss Triggs' stubborn dedication, pushing me at times to always do more and stay focused, I have learned to take charge and to know that I have the tools and strength to get the job done. I then found myself doing community events, helping the community through 8 Days of Hope, Slow Roll Buffalo (healing and connecting with the community through bike riding), and facilitating Erie County Restorative Justice healing circles.

It is through the circles that I met Kelly Whitfield, the founder of The Healing Hub of New York. We talked and discovered we shared the passion of wanting to heal our community through breaking cycles with hope, love, and nourishment. Kelly is an amazing woman who has suffered from many traumas, and God laid this mission on her to create a space to break generational cycles that cause trauma. I joined her in healing Fridays, where we feed over 300 people weekly at times between our two food drives, nutritious lunches, clothing, personal products, essentials, and information on how to connect to services. We prepare the lunches from our homes, many times using our own money. Still, it seems that when we are in need, someone will come along and donate what is needed to carry on this mission. The community has so many caring people who donate in one way or another. The power of faith and prayer is strong in the service of others in our communities.

I dream of blessings for The Healing Hub of New York to receive the funding and grant writers so we can continue blessing lives in ways that will bring love and healing to all those in our communities who suffer from trauma. I had a heavy heart, being aware that there are so many hurting individuals in this world; thinking of the large number is overwhelming. In our community, so many are walking around suffering without a dream or sense of direction as to where to go in life. They are so lacking in hope that they have become clueless that their life is in their own hands, just like I had been for so many years. Once I began to heal and started to dream. I wanted to do what I could to encourage others. After the initial conversation with Kelly, my passion, determination, and dreaming of what the mission could do in our communities was on fire to get started immediately. I knew I wanted to join forces with her, that God led us to each other. It was one of the truly positive relationships to come out of the scary times of quarantine from COVID-19.

I completed the dream of writing this book just prior to COVID. As an essential worker, mother, wife, and so much more, I did not get the forced shut-in memo. My life was hectic as usual, but I now had a front-row seat to the urgency of the needs of others. I suddenly found myself unable to sleep at night, I was called to stand up and get this book typed and ready for print. I took the action steps to make this dream a reality, staying up to the wee hours of the night editing. Thank God to my husband, Julia, Therese, Debbie, and my other loved ones for encouraging me to keep moving on this journey, and to Jennifer, who pushed me to get my book done and stop procrastinating. I am grateful for the honesty from Michelle and my sons for telling me to bleed on it and tell your story. Anyone who knows you will know you always come from a place of love. Grateful for my daughter's support and proofreading, telling me to use things we have said will help, and being ok with me telling the story to help bring healing. Grateful for the blessing God sent me when I was about to have a meltdown because things were not going as I wanted but playing out just as God planned. He sent me my beautiful editor, Debbie, who has blessed me in so many ways. My awesome publisher always says we are in God's time, and you are becoming a better writer through this challenge; I am grateful and dreaming bigger.

I dream that this book will keep hope alive and help hurting people learn self-care and self-love, as I did after being knocked down. I also dream of encouraging all those I encounter to pursue their dreams so that when they read my book, they will use it as a vehicle to assist them in getting where they want to go.

My dream of helping at least one person to relate is extended to all. I don't pretend to be an expert because I am not, but I have a love and empathy for hurting people. I have begun to love myself again and now feel good about life. Focusing on my dream of writing helped me begin to heal my life. I began to open my heart and release the pain of life.

This all started as I began pouring out my emotions writing in my journals. My pain became my healing because I was able to learn from my failures and mistakes in a way I had never done before. I was able to release my fear and frustrations with others and the world without exploding and hurting anyone.

Dreaming of ways to assist in the healing of our world is always what I daydream of. I know it may seem hard to believe, but one night, I was having a conversation with God, angrily telling him that someone needs to do something to help people heal from all the anger and fear going on. I was writing in a crazed, angry way, telling him something needed to be done. Our kids were suffering, in fear, programmed {through video games} to kill, steal, treat women disrespectfully, and not knowing how to have a real conversation, and our world seems to have gone crazy. There is so much happening all the time. I was angry and more frustrated than ever before. Suddenly I heard, "I'm waiting for you. Write the book." I suddenly knew why I couldn't sleep. Writing a book was a dream of mine, but I never had the time to think about it. If I wanted to get back to sleeping like a baby, I needed to begin that dream. It would mean being up for long hours because it would be done after work. My dream would take away from my sleep, and it would be worth it because sharing my lessons would be utilized for good.

I have many dreams. This book is only one of them and is the beginning of how I am choosing to give love to the world while being of service to many. Step one was learning to love me again. I now perceive self-care and self-love as having to come first. When we learn how to love ourselves, we teach others how to love us. This book is my gift to me and all those who dare to dream. Dreams can come true if you are willing to dream and then put in the action steps to make it happen for you.

I AM VALUABLE

I am valuable too, and what I have to give is important
to our world's progress.

It took me time to understand, and I now believe I am worthy and I am valuable to our world. I believe I am connected to all that is, and what I value is necessary for someone else to grow. Our world needs more people to stand up, believe in their value, and help humanity find its worth. Many hurting people are walking around with low or no self-esteem, they're feeling unworthy and as if they don't belong. They walk around thinking that what they have to offer doesn't matter because they screwed up a time or two or even a hundred.

Some are still making mistakes because they can't handle the harsh judgments and critical world in which we live. They may have been abused and mistreated as children, growing up being told they are useless, bad, and good for nothing. They then begin searching for love in all the wrong places, still feeling ignored, like they do not exist. These are the people who society has tossed away in shame. The same people we see in our streets. I have always felt that everyone needs love, and what I have learned is we all matter, and each one of us is valuable. No matter where you are in your life, or what you have done, you matter.

People have become so judgmental and seem to feel a need to always point out what someone else has not done right. As a result, many people will not take a risk. They don't really live, they simply exist. I know this because I was so embarrassed after being hit and mistreated by that police officer in front of my neighbors and loved ones. I sincerely believed that my neighbors thought less of me, that I deserved that treatment, and that I was not worthy of respect. Being racially discriminated against and humiliated led me to believe for many years that I was not valuable. Even though there was one much older woman who reached out to me to tell me she was so sorry for what had happened and that she was there for me. I did take her up on that offer, as I moved out of the town 4 days later. My friends and family rallied together to get us out of there quickly.

This has stuck with me for many years. I was blessed to be able to move to an area that was safer for me and my children. Still, my heart was so heavy as I thought to myself, how many others have not been able to leave an area where they were/are hated because of the color of their skin or how they look?

Quieting myself in meditation and connecting to God by taking deep breaths and grounding myself allows me to navigate through in peace from a place of love. I firmly began to understand I am not the things people have done to me or said about me. I am not my mother or my father. They were just the vehicle God used to bring me here. I am who God created me to be; only I can say who that is. I am valuable. TI am still believing that I am blessed and highly favored. I am here with a purpose and a job to do. I now believe we are all valuable and have gifts planted within us to bring forth. I do now believe our value is truly our gift to humanity.

WHAT YOU STAND FOR
I believe holding on to what you value is
needed to keep us grounded.

After going through years of obstacles, it took me time to understand that I am worthy. I am the person who sets the standards in my life. I did not always realize that it was me who decided what I valued as my truth. It took time for me to wrap my head around this and then to teach myself to embrace the realization that I am a person who deserves respect. The hurt that was done to me when I was racially discriminated against was not who I am. It was a horrible event that took place in my life. This incident caused me and my family and loved ones a lot of pain and suffering. The tears would not stop at times and seeing my baby's face repeatedly in my mind had me stuck. For the first time in my life, I had no self-esteem or drive to do anything.

I knew if I eventually wanted others to respect me, I better begin to learn to give love to myself again. I knew I was perfectly capable, yet I wasn't doing it. It felt like I was just drifting. I began to volunteer; I always did what I could for others and realized I could lose myself in that feeling. There was such a good feeling that came with helping others. I thought to myself, "Imagine what you could do if you gave love to yourself first?" Then that voice in my head repeated the negative words said by the haters, "You can't, it won't matter anyway, don't bother!" Listening to Mom, who guided me back to prayer and meditation, was what assisted me in beginning to give love to me.

Not being sure of what I stand for made it difficult for me. I knew I had to get clear on what was important to me. I guess I was afraid of what people would think if I started to focus on myself. Well, it never mattered to me before in the past what others thought of me, so I made up my mind that it wasn't about to continue just because I was mistreated by that police officer and made to feel humiliated and worthless. Yes, life was hard. I had failed at being a wife, I was a divorced woman, and I have made mistakes, suffered through racial discrimination, and been kicked by life and knocked down, but it was not the end of the world. I had to learn how to get back up stronger. I needed to start somewhere, and right here seemed to be as good a time as any to begin.

I spent many years putting everyone else first. It is my turn; my new standard is self-care and self-love. I am finally acknowledging myself. Self-care and self-love are my new number one standard. Self-care and self-love are the most important. I now see that it is only after I first take care of myself that I truly know how to take care of others. I realized that people will try to mold me into what they feel I should be. If I allow it, but it starts with me, nurturing my spirit, mind, and body first, grounding myself allows me the peace of mind needed to handle life's struggles. I can then act from a place of love instead of reacting out of fear.

Setting the standard is what I choose to do; doing that allows me the freedom to embrace myself with love by nurturing my mind, body, and spirit, and starting from a good place allows me also to make healthier decisions. Giving love to self first gave me the courage to take pride in the person God has blessed me to be, faults and all. Knowing what I stand for and value in life allows me to stand up for what I believe in. Not allowing others to force their beliefs on me. I stand for peace, love, joy, happiness, and kindness to humanity.

I realized my purpose was to be captivating and build humanity, one step at a time, helping people understand that we are one family, God's family. I am not trying to force anything on you, the reader. This is what I believe as my truths; I now focus on what I am here to do on this earth. I believe my purpose is to bring love in wondrous ways back into the lives of everyone I encounter. Recognizing there was a break in my heart. That heartbreak caused it to be easy for anger and angry people to move into my circle. As they say, birds of a feather flock together. I have learned when we are in pain, we act out of it

While I acquired some new tools from reading books to help me. I was thrilled to have mentors I could learn from who were giving me the courage to begin again. I was finally going in a new direction and fearlessly taking each gift of a new day, as the gift that it is. I am enjoying every moment, giving love to self-first, life and those who will accept it. I choose to be a part of healing hearts. I am bringing love to everything that I do. I stand for love, self-care, and self-love. I believe we can be kind to others when we can give love to ourselves.

BUTTERFLY
I believe we are all important and responsible for helping our world evolve.

Life has taught me that we grow and learn through stages and seasons. Each stage of our life is vital to the next stage. We must find the lesson life is trying to teach us to rise. Understanding where we are right now is necessary to propel us into our next phase. Perceiving where we are is not where we will remain. If I receive the lesson God is trying to teach me, I will blossom like a butterfly, then grow and morph into the next phase of life. I now conclude that there are no mistakes in life. Better choices are to be made, and our job is to make the best choice for every situation. We are here to grow and learn.

I felt shame for years, afraid of what people and the Church would think of me. Being what I thought at the time, a failure because a divorced woman was frowned upon. I had listened to sermons - worshiped, and read in the bible (not understanding repentance at that time), just believing what I had done was bad. I was so hurt and afraid of being judged. I punished myself for many years. Like a butterfly, I stayed in my protective cocoon and would not allow love in. I now comprehend when we are in a dark place, we tend to punish ourselves. We are being our own worst enemy. We try to be perfect because of the brainwashing of life. I now perceive that we must understand we are all just ordinary people, and we do make mistakes.

This has most of us stuck in fear. Not knowing which way to go or how to deal with what life has handed us. I found safety in a butterfly. Holding on to fear and refusing to forgive kept me stuck. Not comprehending that I am the key to my destiny, it was not until I allowed myself to release the guilt. This helped to free me from the cage I had around my heart. Grateful, I now see that every day I wake up is an opportunity to spread my wings. I am giving love, growing into the next phase of life, and watering the seeds that God has placed deep within me. Imagining life, I want to live as I see it. I believe we must be the courage for someone else as we live our life's story, being our best selves.

When we practice self-care and self-love, we help others to see through us that we are in the driver's seat of our own lives. After reading and following advice from my mentors, I believe it is up to us to open our hearts. So we can allow love in. Embracing life and the hard times allows us to spread our wings like butterflies. We then can allow life to take us where we need to go. I am so grateful for God, my mother, Oprah, Lisa Nichols, Mel Robbins, Brenee

Brown, Louise Hayes, Bob Proctor, and my many self-development mentors, who helped me along my journey, helping me blossom into a butterfly. I am forever a learner, a work in progress.

BELIEVE
I now perceive that life is whatever you say it is.

It was not until the moment when I feared for both my and my son's life, faced with the unknown outcome, that I chose to believe. I believed if I called on the name of "Jesus" my heavenly father would protect us in that moment of uncertainty. While this angry police officer proceeded to perform in a way I had never witnessed, I asked why this officer would react in such a hateful, harmful way without even asking me any questions or giving me a chance to speak. I taught my children the police were here to protect and serve us, the people. Just as my family had taught me.

At that moment, my child and I were confused about why this was not what we were witnessing. The officer hit me several times, calling me the "n-word, black b**, and screamed, do I know who he is? As he stood in front of my home, he repeatedly asked if I knew the town name – his way of telling me I didn't belong in that primarily white town – and told me to go back where I belonged. Undeniably, this was a misunderstanding of some sort. I had lived in that town for years, and it was, until this moment, a wonderful experience. I encountered many amazing police officers. None of them ever said anything out of line. They were always very nice and helpful. No matter where we are in life, there are bad seeds in every bunch, I do believe.

Before I moved there, a few co-workers who had experienced racial profiling in the past had mentioned the town police were "bigots" and that I needed to be careful of the police, but I had never had any issues. This had me shaken. I was in shock. I was badly depressed because of this situation. I was totally out of it for years. It had me in a deep depression. It was so hard to function, and I struggled to keep it together for my children. This incident had us all depressed, and my son was also attacked, so I knew he was struggling with his emotions. He probably felt guilty on top of his other emotions because he ran to me for help, and then I was attacked. I wanted to disappear, and I know he did too, but I refused to leave my babies without their mother.

This situation was very traumatic, and it sent us all spiraling in directions that were unknown. Court hearings dragged on because of rescheduling, and there were so many different appointments to attend that had to be squeezed into our already hectic schedules. It was at that moment when I realized I was truly much stronger than I thought. My strength came from allowing the pain. Trusting and believing in my faith, God will bring me whatever I need to weather the storms of life.

Believing the God within talks to us when we take the time out to be still after many years of suffering through this traumatic experience that took place. I began to connect with my breath in meditation. Hoping to be guided in the way I should go. Trusting that God makes no mistakes and is allowing this painful situation for a reason. This moment, too, shall pass. I believed that in time, I would be better from this, and my son and our family would heal and move on. It was after several conversations with my mother. It took me years to snap out of the depression this caused to my son, my family, and me. Honestly, it was forgiving the officer first, then believing I was worthy. My sons are worthy of having an amazing life. I am not in that situation. It was simply a bad event that took place in my life. I can move past this and begin a new chapter in life.

What other people believe about me is not important. It is only what I believe that matters. Bad things happen to good people all the time. I do not believe this lesson was for me. It was for my loved ones to see that it is not what happens to us; it is truly what we do after that makes the difference as to how our life will go. The reaction we choose to utilize on how we will move forward. I could have chosen to handle this with anger and hate. My family's life trajectory would have worsened, and more painful situations would have occurred. We have had so much pain. I decided to forgive and give love to me.

Therefore, my decision could begin a new direction for my family and me. The healing process could start with me. I always believe that God will work it out instead of stressing and trying to be vengeful and handling it myself. Believe I am a gift to our world, and the God within me is leading me to fulfill my purpose here if I allow it and embrace what is with love instead of hate. It is whatever you say it is, and I believe. My family's pain is turning into healing for us and those whom we love. We will no longer run but face our challenges head-on, believing in our faith. As I said, it starts with me giving love to myself first and then to everyone and everything I encounter. I believe this is a good place to begin our healing.

MAGNETISM
We all have a choice as to what we give out.

As I stated before, it was Bob Proctor who got me to think correctly. Only when I listened to his audio did I begin to watch closely what I was putting out. I began monitoring my mouth and my thoughts. Trying my best to be more positive because, after my divorce, this was not easy to do; I gave nothing because I felt that I had nothing to give. Being heartbroken hurts so badly, honestly, I don't wish this pain on anyone. My heart was under lock and key, and I was just floating through life.

Allowing the television to set the tone, depending on the show and the numerous commercials. Once I understood that what radiates from our hearts determines what happens in our lives. Knowing we are the power in our world, I decided to radiate joy, love, and peace. I did this before my divorce and life traumas, unconsciously, because it came naturally to me. It was my broken heart and the pain of my divorce that caused me to shift from love to anger and then the series of life events that took place after. I was guilty of closing my heart out of fear of being hurt again.

I try not to watch violent programs because I do not feel good after the show is over, especially if it is a horrific one. I usually would have nightmares, and in my dreams, I was the victim. I was angry, going through the struggles I was watching, and I attracted angry people. It was exhausting, and I decided the drama/horror genre was to be limited and began watching more uplifting and educational shows. I found I was more energetic watching uplifting television and movies and was in a better mood; I also found I was attracting a more gentle type of people.

Now, even more importantly, I realize that I am like a magnet. I do believe that whatever I give out, I will receive back. Mother always told us this, but now it is being taught by great motivators. So, it must be true. Sorry, Mom, for not getting this sooner.

With that being said, I am now choosing to be in love, the love I wish to see in the world for humanity choosing to radiate unconditional love to everyone. Now I understand that if I do not wish to see it figuratively at my front door, I better not speak it or let it cross my lips. It was hard at first, but I had to do something different if I wanted to experience something different in my life and my children's lives. I had to allow myself to change what I was sending out into the universe. To do this, I had to close my mouth.

I promised there would be No more wishing anything evil on anyone, no matter how mean or nasty they have been to me or my loved ones. Trust in due time, God will work everything out even when my life starts special, in a way I did not plan or expect it to go. It is up to me to make a conscious decision to change, stop, take three deep breaths, and begin to train myself to bring about a positive change. Take me to a happy place by putting a smile in my heart. From remembering something that brought me joy or happiness. Beginning my day connecting with my higher power, radiating love before I start every day. I now believe this will magnetize to me and our world love.

DISCIPLINE
Learning to be disciplined is hard.

Learning to be disciplined was and still is one of the hardest things I have tried to do in life. It is a continuous battle I struggle with. It is easy to say what needs to be done, write it down, and think about it, but doing it is something else. We know what needs to be done and can tell others what they need to do for themselves, too. It is so easy that it is hard. I went back and forth for years trying to get in control of myself when I began this journey to healing my life, and to this day, I still have issues that need work. I have taken so many different roads trying to figure it out. What I have come to see is that there is no perfect way on this journey, you must find out what works for you. When you figure out how you work best at things, create a daily habit you know you will have no problem forcing yourself to do. Doing this helped me to come out of my comfort zone.

I would start something several times and then quit and start again before I finally got it. I still have issues with things but I know I am not going to quit. I will do that thing until it becomes a part of who I am. I know who I am now, and who I am is beautiful. I did not always feel good about myself when I was in that very dark place. I did not care to think of how to be better at doing the things needed. I was just lucky I felt like doing anything at all. Trying to get me to be "disciplined", was not even a thought. I now understand that feeling good helps, especially when you are trying to make life happen.

I am grateful and have decided to take each day as it comes. I know I am not perfect and that anything good does take time and is worth working on. Discipline will come to me as I learn to set up the path for success. It does not matter how many times I fall and fail; it may happen several times before I get the thing I am currently working on. The only thing that matters is that I keep trying until I succeed, ensuring I do what brings me joy along the way. Acknowledging to myself that just when I think I have it all handled, something else may pop up out of nowhere to take me off course. I understand that the discipline I have just set up is the tool to help me learn how to navigate my way through and stay on course, as it helps to take me where I need to go.

I have learned that most of the time, discipline is what I need to get the job done. Once I conquer that challenge after I have learned discipline in my challenge I usually find I am rising to a new level in my life. This only happens after I truly learn the lesson God was trying to teach me. It seems as if there is absolutely no way of getting around the pain in our lives we must go through to receive our blessings. I now choose to go through with peace, being grounded as I learn self-care and self-love along the way.

TRANSFORMING LIVES

It is enlightening to learn that our actions affect one another.

As I drifted back through some of my life obstacles and began sifting through what happened, I could now see that this was a time of crisis. I was overwhelmed because too many things were taking place at once. My emotions were flying high, and I was not thinking about how my actions and words would affect someone else.

Now, I can see how actions and words impact how others react to me. I started realizing that thinking before reacting was not on my mind at all. Usually, I acted out immediately, doing whatever I felt was needed to fill the void of pain. There was never a thought of the past or what would happen in the future. I lived in the now, and only that moment in time mattered.

Desperately, searching to numb my heartache while I was upset and going through some of the toughest, most challenging times, I now know things I have done and said were not always good. I had to learn that the hard way. Coming from a hurting place, you are not always your best self. I do now believe this after learning from my many mistakes. We need to make it our business to watch what we do and say, especially in the presence of young minds. I pray that each of us is aspiring to be an example that transforms the young and the old.

Remember that we are all a continuous work in progress, and we will make mistakes, fall, fail, and mess up. I now see It is important to be conscious of our actions, and intensely focus on trying to make the best decision for the moment we are in at the time. Learning how to get back up when we fail. We can then begin being the example of what we would like to see: leaving a remarkable impression wherever we are—hoping that when we fall short. We can own it by taking on accountability and moving through the challenge with love. Understanding that our very actions transform lives. It is not always what you say that makes the difference. It is your actions taken, seen, and taught to those watching on the sidelines.

When they see you correct your mistakes and see you work on getting better each time, somehow, it makes it easy for others to realize they can, too. It encourages others to know it is ok to screw up. No one is perfect. I believe we need to get up and try again in a different way. Transforming your life and others and encouraging others to "believe" it is possible to keep getting better. It is true that one good thing brings another. Each one of us is connected to this universe. I believe we all matter, and what we do matters too. I do now "believe" it is not just important but necessary to act from a place of love.

Becoming a part of the continuous transformation of our world, after reading and listening to my mentors, I would then begin to meditate, connect, and ground myself. I believe we grow in enlightenment and wisdom, then rise higher and become who God created us to be. After I listened to the Oprah and Tony Robbins interview on Super Soul Conversations EP# 12, I realized it is important to watch and listen carefully to be present with others. We need to put down our phones and perceptions and just listen, see, and hear what others are saying, even if they are saying through actions, not words.

This helped me to learn that we are all here experiencing suffering to some degree. I believe it is up to us to acknowledge where we are in life so that we can start from there and find what works for us and begin to transform into our best selves. We also need to stop beating ourselves up if what worked for someone else doesn't work for us. We each have our own journey, and must find what works for us, as individuals.

I was so excited to learn that both Tony and Oprah are real people, just like me. They believe some of the things that I believe that we need to change our state of mind. They both experienced horrible traumas in life, but here they were having a conversation, which was so normal and like I might have with someone I am close to. They were no longer the wealthy, successful, inspiring celebrities we all know; they were just two people having an open conversation.

Watching and listening to them, I realized I could face my fears and make things happen. If they could do it, so could I. They were vulnerable and open, and though my experiences are different from theirs, we all experience pain, trauma, and challenges in life. We all make mistakes. I decided I could write a book about my journey, about my healing, and maybe someone will read my story and say, "If she can do it, I can, too," just as I did after listening to that podcast. If I talk about my mistakes and how I have grown, my loved ones and strangers will see that mistakes do not define who you are, it is how you rise from them that determines where you are. I also realize there isn't a timeline to being your best self – it is a constant work in progress.

HAPPINESS
Happiness is what I choose. It has become my truth.

Intensely acknowledging all the problems and goings-on in our world every day, some major event is shaping and molding someone's life in a new direction. If I chose to focus on the negativity as I did in the past, I could easily slip back into depression. I learned that it is so very important to wake up and choose how my day will go. Starting with the choice to be happy. This is my way of living life now. It wasn't always, but it works. Thanks to Mom, Oprah Winfrey, Bob Proctor, Jack Canfield, Les Brown, and my many mentors, who have helped me begin my day in a state of happiness.

I have learned to fill my heart with so much joy, there is no room for fear to set in. Living a joy-filled, happy life. I am getting healthier every day. I almost can't believe it after all I have been through. While having a conversation, a dear friend said to me once, "I refuse to settle for the bull." After our conversation, I thought to myself, I did not even realize I had been settling. Being in a dark place in life had my mind in a fog. I understand happiness is a choice. I recognize now that I must choose what I want to see in my life, or anything can happen.

I know this to be true because it was how I lived my life for years. Happiness was not even a thought. I was paralyzed and terrified to allow myself to feel. I was so afraid of being hurt. Now, when I am around negative people or going through a negative time, I do not allow the negative energy to take over my thoughts and life. Instead, I meet them where they are, listen with concern and love, and give what I can – within my boundaries – to help. I then can walk away, knowing that I did what I could without hurting myself or my loved ones.

Therefore, we can help each other to rise. If they are not positive, happy people, I will keep my conversation short but give love anyway and be that ear for them to bounce things off. Getting out quickly and not allowing any of "their" negativity to penetrate me, I understand I am only in control of myself, and no longer will I just allow others to influence me with toxicity.

I choose to experience my life with laughter and happily dance my way through. I practice giving love and kindness to all I encounter, enjoying every day as if it were my last. Often, I am asked, "What drug are you on? You're too happy. I need some of that". They look at me like I am crazy. Some even look at me angrily, telling me I am living in a bubble. What others think about me is none of my business. I have learned not to accept those opinions; they are angry at me because of what they won't do or want for themselves. I can't help them or me if I become just like them, spouting out anger.

That has never been me - judging others does not make me happy. It does not even feel good. I had my share of being a part of the conversations while others were trash-talking someone else who was not in the room to defend themselves. Although I said nothing, it still left a sour feeling in my soul. I choose to stay in my lane, not judge others for what they do, look in my mirror, and be happy and grateful for all my blessings. I am not here to judge anyone. I am here to line up with the plan God has for me. Allowing others to be who they are and live the life that works for them.

I am no longer staying focused on negativity but choosing to be happy. I am embracing new concepts to our world's problems by being a part of the solution and helping to change our world for the better. It starts with me being at peace in the middle of this storm called life. Happiness is a choice, and I choose to be happy.

LOVE
We all desire love, and love is many different things.

Love can be kind, forgiving, and unconditional. Love can be strong or weak in a moment of trial. Love can be many different experiences, and it hurts sometimes. Love is the sun in the sky, the air that I get to breathe, or a moonlight walk watching the stars that shine oh so bright. Love is the smile on my child's face, the laughter of my life partner. Love is my dog rushing to my side as I sneeze to make sure I am ok. Love is my cat, jumping in my lap first thing in the morning, giving me another reason to smile.

Love is our family and the beautiful way they come together when challenges arise, no questions asked. They are just there, with arms wide open, giving unconditional love.

Love is my fiancé, choosing to step out of his comfort zone, getting married in the family church (on my dad's side of the family) on our wedding day, in front of our family, friends, and loved ones, when he is an introvert and does not like being around a lot of people, and as he was suffering from dehydration and lack of nutrition. He did all of this to prove to me how much he loves me in front of our family. He was falling apart inside, nervous, scared, and having an anxiety attack, risking the chance of being embarrassed. I told him we did not have to have a big wedding, but he insisted, he also believed it was important for our families and friends to witness our vows in front of God.

Love is the joy of a hug from a special friend whom you haven't seen or talked to for years, but you know they will always be there with open arms and an open heart. Knowing that when you call, they will answer.

Love is rushing to the side of a lifelong friend who just lost his dad, knowing you can't do much because you're married now, but taking the time to teach him how to release the pain that life has given him through breathing and meditation.

Love is lying by a beautiful fireplace, next to someone special, with whom you have shared life experiences that you will cherish for a lifetime. Love is forgiving a friend that you used to date for, not just being ok with just being a friend because life took us in different directions.

Love is someone who you know loves you and cares for your well-being. It is someone who will always be in your corner to uplift, elevate and encourage you, and is truly a friend to you. Love is letting go without judgment because a friend wanted more, and your sincere friendship was not enough in moments of life's struggles.

Love is forgiving him for wanting an FWB (friend with benefits) at this moment because that is what both of you were used to in the past before you got back with the man who is now your husband. Life has moved, and now, the things you used to do, you no longer do. We grow in life and things we used to love to do we learn we must let go and allow God to guide us in new ways. Blessing us to love and live a healthy life on our new path.

Love is a stranger who goes out of their way to help just because they know in their gut it is the right thing to do. Love is doing something for someone else in your moment of struggle and being a blessing for them.

Love is a moment of silence, taking deep breaths, connecting to my higher power, who meets all my needs. Love is a hike with friends or a walk in the park holding hands with the one you love. Love is breakfast in bed made by your children or partner. Love is quality time with your lover, loved ones, or besties, doing whatever feels good at the moment, knowing all that matters is that you are together, giving love and support in our times of need, and encouraging one another to keep moving forward.

Love is being there for the special events that take place in life. Understanding that you do not like or care for what you are experiencing, but the event is important to the one you love; therefore, you will be there supporting, giving love, and kindness. Love is giving my full attention as we have a conversation, and you know that I am not preoccupied with other things while talking to me; I am present. Love is you, giving me your undivided attention, being present with me at this moment, and helping me understand that I am important to you. Love is knowing the things I enjoy and doing some of them with me. Love is a risk, and it is many things to different people, but it is worth it.

CONFIDENCE

We do not always feel good about who we are.

For many years, it was very challenging for me. I did not feel good about who I had become. Being depressed had caused me to lack the self-esteem I once had. This caused me to begin eating so much that I almost became a glutton, consuming huge amounts of sugary foods and drinks. Every night for years, I was not conscious of what I was inhaling or the time I was doing it. Doing this would make me feel good and satisfy my taste buds for a while.

Food is love, and it was just what I needed at the time to help me feel confident. Sugar was not going to break my heart. I desperately needed to feel good because I was struggling on every level. Life had me in its grip and I was drowning.

I had lost confidence, and I felt like a failure. It was difficult to trust my judgments, so I didn't. Life just happened. I had no clue where I was headed, and not one thought about my direction entered my mind. I was stuck in fear and did not mind standing still. Steeped in challenges and depression, I would sit on that couch day after day watching television. I was listening here and there to it because I didn't know what was on it; I guess it was on for background noise only. One day, a Phen-Phen commercial came on; it grabbed my attention, and I stopped and listened. I had heard it can help obese individuals. I thought to myself, "Am I obese?" Not in my eyes, but I felt heavy, and my clothes were snug.

I wore stretchy pants all the time; it was getting hard to move, and I had no confidence. Noticing I had not ever been this large, not ever, not even when I was pregnant, I called my doctor to schedule an appointment. I could not get in, but I heard from friends there was a doctor at BGH. Who had a program for those who were ready to follow a healthier diet, exercise, and be willing to improve their life? Phen-Phen was the latest craze. I was not a person to take any drugs. It was not my thing, but I could, for a short time, do this program and these diet pills. Being monitored by a doctor, I was desperate and told myself, "This would be for a little while", not forever. I was hoping it would jump-start my life and build my confidence, propelling me in a new direction.

My weight, along with the weight of life, had become too much. I was overwhelmed. No longer could I just let things happen. I had enough. My weight had spiraled from 140 pounds to two hundred and fifteen. I needed to pay attention to what I was allowing in my body, to become aware of what time I was eating and set up some goals. Having no confidence in me, it was so hard to do anything. So, I made the call, my appointment day came up, and I talked my aunt into going with me. Both she and I struggled with our weight issues. We met with the doctor. He explained this is not a permanent fix. We will begin Phen-Phen for three months, along with Prozac for depression. Together, these will work side by side as tools to help us gain control of our eating habits and lives. We would also be establishing and implementing good habits to live a healthier life.

Right after the consultation we were examined and monitored for three months. We exercised and developed better eating habits. The weight began to fall off and as I looked better, I started to feel better. My confidence did go up for a while, but I did not pay attention to why I was depressed. It was not long before I was right back where I started, needing to lose weight again. It was not until years later that I realized that the weight we carry on our bodies is truly the weight of life.

This cycle for me went on for many years as I tried several diets, doctors, and other fads. That would last for a moment, leaving me larger and having to lose more weight the next time. It was not until I decided to pray and meditate, being grateful for what I have, connecting with God within first, and going back to what Mom taught us as children, that I gained my confidence. It was just that simple, I couldn't believe it. I had tried just about everything to build my confidence.

Instead of filling the empty void with things that harmed me, I now choose to connect with my spirit, embracing what it is and allowing God to work through me as I nurture my mind, body, and spirit. Creating a routine and listening to positive affirmations and spiritual and motivational speakers who are uplifting has helped me live a life being calm and in peace instead of chaos and fear.

My Pastor Jerimiah Carter, Cindi Trimm, TD Jakes, Joyce Meyers, Joel Osteen, Charles Stanley, and Dr. Bill Winston were some of my favorite faith teachers, helping me grow and continue on my faith journey, connecting with my spirit. Dr Bill Winston, thank you for your Walking by Faith series. It is also one of my favorites. I now know that the church lives in me. What a confidence booster that is! Understanding who we are made a big difference in how I thought about things, too.

Thank you, Dr. Cindi Trimm, for laying that out in your motivational prayer Who You Are 2017 mp4. I am forever grateful; it was like a light switch went on as I listened to it several times, smiling bigger and bigger each time and becoming more and more confident. It assisted in giving me the strength to begin again. Yes, I still have moments when I slip, but I now allow the slip. Then I sit in silence, asking what can I learn?

As I have learned from self-development teachings, I ask myself, what is God within trying to teach me? I then sit, wait, and review the situation. Believing that from this situation, only good will come. Trusting in my faith, I am now confident God is where my help comes from, and I am divinely guarded and protected. No longer do I have a problem with being confident or filling my void with crap. I now watch what I allow in. Believing I must give love to all three: my mind, body, and spirit. If I choose to live my best life with confidence.

BLESSED
Feeling blessed is truly the way to go through life.

There were years, months, days, minutes, and seconds that I woke up not understanding how truly blessed I am. I now believe every day that I wake up is a blessing. When I was filled with toxic negative thinking, negativity was truly all that came out of my mouth. Filled with so much negative energy surrounding me it was clogging my mind. Indeed, good things can't come when you are filled with bad thinking. If I wanted to see something new for me, and I did, I had to do things differently.

I had to begin to count my blessings. It was tough at first to find the good. I started with my home, looking around me at all that God had given me - free of charge. It was then that I could see that I was truly living an abundantly blessed life already. I am blessed with the sun, the moon, and the stars, just enough air to keep me breathing and alive. I am blessed with water, heat, and electricity. I am blessed with my beautiful home and all its amenities. I am blessed with a vehicle that allows me to take my loved ones wherever they need to go.

I continued looking at my blessings:

Blessed with clothing, furniture, blankets, and pillows.

Blessed with coats, boots, sneakers, and shoes.

Blessed with my beautiful heart that allows me to love.

I am blessed with good health; this is a huge blessing! Good health is wealth. This allows me to do whatever I want. I am filled with so much energy to go to and from my destinations. I am blessed to exercise my beautiful body in fun-loving ways such as walking, running, biking, hiking, dancing, etc. While I continue to work on improving the parts of me that need more love. After just going over the things I saw around me, and there were many more, I could begin to see I was blessed. I started to feel a little different, thinking I did have so much to be grateful for and maybe it was time to work on the things that I could control.

FEAR TO FAITH

I was in fear for at least a decade, traveling through this journey called life. I was fumbling my way through and trying to do things on my own. As I held onto my fear, I struggled in every area of my life. Feeling fear is something out of this world. You never know what is coming next, and, feeling scared, I would not know how to handle it. This is not a good way to wake up or to end your day.

I had to find a healthy way to navigate through my day-to-day tasks. I wanted to always be a good example not only for my children but also for any child or adult I come in contact with. I had lived this nightmare for so long that I wasn't sure I could change. I was at the point in my life where I was ready to make a serious change. I needed to take myself from fear to faith, but how? Fear had me, and it truly led me every step.

My health was not good, my finances were in shambles, my relationship was on shaky ground, and honestly, I could go on for days about what was not right in my life. My faith had been something I used to do, not something I truly believed. As a child, I knew I always felt better when I prayed, so I decided to start there. Prayer and being grateful were two things I had not practiced in years. I was too angry at the world to do that.

I began each day in prayer, nothing big, just reading the twenty-third, twenty-seventh, and ninety-first Psalms. Some days, I would read all three; others, it would be just one. I would then sit, silently breathing, connecting with my breath, and thanking God for all I am blessed with. I remember how my mother taught us to meditate while teaching us positive ways to release our frustrations and fears. I started feeling a little better each day. Then, I began listening to audiobooks from some of the best motivators. As I started to feel good about myself, I began to think of them as my mentors. I decided that if they could go from nothing to something, then just maybe, I could, too. I thought about how bad I felt for so many years. I knew there were others who did as well. Then, it hit me: maybe I could help someone else take their life from fear to faith, too. I desperately wanted to help, to spare others from being stuck in fear.

I am not a doctor. I do not pretend to be an expert, but I do know that I took my life back, and I wanted to share my story. I needed to. I began to live again, and every day continues to get better for me. I want to share this gift of love with my loved ones and others. I am hopeful that it will help bring healing to others, by shifting their life from fear to faith. I now have very strong faith, and I am always continuing to rise. I believe that my decision to build a relationship with God by building a morning routine helped me to move through challenges with love instead of fear.

ACKNOWLEDGEMENTS

This book is dedicated to my children, James, Johnathan, Donnie, Penny, and Jessica, who have always been very supportive of me as I embark on my mission of giving love to everyone and everything I come in contact with. My children have shared me with many projects, committees, and organizations. They never complained about giving love, knowing that my mission is to give love to those who feel unlovable. For whatever reason, I have always felt an urgency to connect with those who feel left out. I am grateful for my children. Thank you all for your support. I love and adore each one of you. And always know, You're my favorite.

To my husband {Owen}, my mother {Little Mamie}, father {Herbert Jr. II} and grandmother {Big Mamie}, my deceased grandparents {Herbert I and Phoebe Gennis) great-great grandmother {Margaret Frank A.K.A Moma}. Thank you for all your wisdom. And to all my in-laws, thank you for embracing me with love.

To my brothers, Lee, Johna, Lil Herbert III, and James, thank you for the many lessons in love. I have learned from you and all the love you give me whenever we are together. Thank you to my sisters, Melissa, Ursula, Peaches, Ginger, Rita, Rebeka, Keoki, Keioana, Monica, Deana, and Deceased Clarese A.K.A Reese. Thank you for all that you are to me and our family. To my Aunt Maggie, Aunt Alice, Aunt Marion, Aunt Louise, Aunt Ginger, Aunt Kathy, Aunt Kimalin, and deceased Aunt Caroline. Thank you for all our encouraging conversations. To my Uncle Tony and Uncle Robert, thank you for always encouraging me to go further. To my other Uncles, thank you for the life lessons learned. To my cousins and extended family, thank you.

To my work family at Emerald-Buffalo Community Healthcare Center, thank you for all the love you have given me over the past twenty years.

To my besties; my sisters from another mother - Julia, Lisa, Jennifer, Jennifer P, Felicia, Dawn, Dee, Therese, Michelle, Antonella, Rosie, Wendy, Rhonda, Diann, Vickie, Joann, Cheryl, Darlene, Debbie, LaCandice, Amy, Dayna, and Catherine your love, support, and friendship have been a constant source of strength for me.

To Habitat for Humanity Buffalo, my Erie County Restorative Justice Coalition family, Voice Buffalo, University Heights Collaborative Board, and Healing Hub of New York family, I am so grateful to work with you. Your dedication and commitment to our shared mission have been truly inspiring. Thank you for accepting me as part of the team.

To my Delaware YMCA family, thank you for all you do for our community. Even when families do not have the funds to afford to pay, they can still attend and have a positive way to release the negative energies of life.

THANK YOU
There are many reasons to give thanks.

Thank you for God's grace. Thank you for waking me today, thank you for the air that I breathe, and thank you for the beautiful body that my spirit gets to live in. Thank you for my eyes, which God has blessed me to see in the world he created. Thank you to my parents, my husband, my children, family, friends, and loved ones. Thank you for my home, Habitat for Humanity Buffalo, and all the family, friends, and volunteers who helped us work on our beautiful home. Thank you for all the wonderful material blessings I have been blessed to put into my home. Thank you for the program that Habitat has made buying a home a possibility for families who have a desire to own their home.

Thank you for the nourishment and the funds to buy it. Thank you for taking the time to do whatever I want to create the life I want. Thank you for all the knowledge that surrounds me and helps me continue to grow. Thank you for my newfound discipline, wisdom, dreams, and encouragement. Thank you for my place of work and for every job I have been blessed to learn from throughout my life. Thank you to all my co-workers who taught me valuable lessons. Thank you for every conversation - good or bad. Thank you for the sun and the moon. Thank you for the stars that shine throughout the universe. Thank you for humanity evolving in wonderful ways as people learn to give love to our world and all the people who dwell in it. Thank you for this abundant life that I get to live in and for the clarity to see all my blessings. Thank you. Thank you. Thank You.

ABOUT THE AUTHOR

Erricka Willard, a native of Buffalo, New York, spent her formative years in the Blackrock section of the city. In 1979, her family relocated to the Westside of Buffalo, a decision driven by her mother's desire for a diverse and safe environment to raise her children. A strong spiritual believer, Erricka's mother instilled a deep faith in her children and fostered a love for the Lord. Despite being a single mother, she created a welcoming environment for her children and their neighborhood friends.

Quality time and most weekends were spent with great-grandma (Moma) or dad for weekend visitations. Usually, in one church or another, both Dad and Moma shared their passion for living a holy life as lovers of our Heavenly Father. She is blessed with a very large and sometimes dysfunctional family, like almost everyone alive.

Erricka felt a great love growing up. The love of her family and close friends is truly what helped her to overcome the many challenges she faced throughout life.

She attended high school and college in Buffalo, New York. She obtained her Business Management Associate's Degree at Bryant & Stratton Business College Institute. After graduating from Lafayette H.S.

She married her high school sweetheart and was instantly blessed as not only a wife but a stepmother, too. Although they were very much in love, the challenges of life became too much to overcome. Overwhelmed with emotions and not knowing how to deal with the pain, their love affair was cut short, and they divorced. Being forced with the challenge of starting over as a single mother had her very depressed and struggling to embrace the many emotions she was desperately trying to keep under control.

Erricka became an advocate for Habitat for Humanity, Buffalo. She advocates for children, including those in the foster care system, the elderly, domestic violence victims, Voice Buffalo, the Erie County Restorative Justice Coalition, and humanity in general. She frequently facilitates and co-facilitates restorative circles and practices.

She is very passionate about community work. She is a member of the University Heights Collaborative Board in her community, which she loves, she is doing all she can to assist in bringing unity and healing as she also volunteers in the community. She is also a part of The Healing Hub of New York as the Food Drive Coordinator and board member, heading up Healing Fridays.

Life can be good when you embrace it and allow "what is."

Printed in the USA
CPSIA information can be obtained
at www.ICGtesting.com
LVHW070805141124
796389LV00020B/453